LIVE LONG
&
STRONG!

LIVE LONG
&
STRONG!

God's Keys to Youth Renewal and Long Life

Derek Walker

EVANGELISTA MEDIA™ srl
Via Maiella, 1
66020 San Giovanni Teatino (Ch)—Italy

"Changing the World, One Book at a Time."

This book and all other Evangelista Media™ and Destiny Image™ Europe books are available at Christian bookstores and distributors worldwide.

To order products, or for any other correspondence:

EVANGELISTA MEDIA™ srl
Via Maiella, 1
66020 San Giovanni Teatino (Ch)—Italy
Tel. +39 085 959806 • Fax: +39 085 9090113
Email: info@evangelistamedia.com

Or reach us on the Internet: www.evangelistamedia.com

ISBN 13: 978-88-97896-98-2
ISBN 13 Ebook: 978-88-97896-85-2

For Worldwide Distribution, Printed in U.S.A.
1 2 3 4 5 6 / 16 15 14 13

CONTENTS

FOREWORD

What a privilege to be asked by my dear friend, Pastor Derek Walker, to write a few words by way of an introduction to his latest book.

I have known Derek for several years and have been deeply blessed by his spirituality, depth of knowledge, and remarkable teaching ministry. When I have struggled to understand certain truths and have turned to him for advice and help, I have never been disappointed and I have learned to trust his counsel and wisdom.

Derek has the uncommon gift of being able to teach about high and sometimes complex concepts in the Lord with clarity that is easily understood. In this latest book, Derek has brought us back to the biblical truth that God wants to bless us with a long and fruitful life. Today's emphasis on healthy eating and living in order to live a long life is incomplete without God's clear instruction in His Word on how to live a long life. This is an important and challenging message coming at a time when the enemy of our souls wants to attack and to cut short the life of God's people.

Recently Billy Graham, at the age of ninety-two, made the statement that he was prepared for death but had never been prepared for old age. In this book, Pastor Derek encourages me, as I grow older, to increasingly depend upon God for my strength; and as I trust Him, I will continue to be useful all the days of my life.

I have been encouraged and strengthened by the wisdom in this book. I encourage you to read it with an open mind and to allow God to speak directly to you, and then to rise up in faith, believing what God says and stand upon His promise of long life. If you do this, I know that you will be blessed in the same way that I have been blessed.

Thank you, Derek, for this timely challenge.

Michael Ross-Watson

Missionary statesman Michael Ross-Watson and his wife, Esther, have served the Lord together for more than forty years. They served as missionaries with WEC International in Indonesia. Michael has been a pastor, teacher, and missions director. He is Honorary Pastor of the large Anglican Church of our Saviour in Singapore.

Introduction

THE QUEST FOR LONG LIFE

From time immemorial humankind has pursued the hope of long life and even immortality. We have a deep desire to live forever, but we are too aware of the aging process and the certainty of death. Where should we go to find answers in the face of this greatest challenge?

It may be a surprise to you that the Bible has a lot to say about living long and strong in this life, as well as receiving eternal life. Jesus, the only one who has conquered death, said, "I am the resurrection and the life" (John 11:25). He did not just come that we might have eternal life in heaven when we die, but that we might enjoy *fullness of life* now. Jesus said, "I have come that they may have *life*, and that they may have it *more abundantly*" (John 10:10).

Do you want to live long and strong? Did you know that God also wants this for you? His will is to bless you with health so that you have a long and fully satisfying life! His promise to all those who put their trust in Him is: "With *long life* I will satisfy him, and show him My salvation" (which includes deliverance from an early death) (Psalm 91:16). God wants to be the source and strength of your life and the length of your days (see Deuteronomy 30:20, Psalm 27:1). His covenant blessings include healing and renewal of youth (see Psalm 103:1-5). God wants our days to be long, and that it be well with us (see Deuteronomy 5:16). He says that by receiving His words of life and wisdom, our days will be multiplied, and the years of our life increased (see Proverbs 9:11). The New Testament confirms these promises are still true for us today: "...you were called to this, that you may inherit a blessing [of long and strong life]. For "He who would *live life and see good days...*" (1 Peter 3:9-10).

Obviously these things do not just drop on us automatically. It is essential that we know and receive these divine promises of youth renewal and long life. Just having a passing acquaintance with them will not make much difference. We must be fully informed and persuaded that they belong to us so that we can partake of the divine life in these precious promises. That is why I have written this book. The information in these pages will lengthen and strengthen your life on earth so that it is not cut short! Although there are many books on healing, this book breaks fresh ground in providing an in-depth study of what the Scriptures have to say about the neglected subject of long life and youth renewal. It will build your faith so that you will be able to declare, "I shall not die young, but live [long], and declare the works of the Lord!" (Psalm 118:17).

This book is designed to help you discover what God's Word says about having a long and strong life. It is written to reveal to your heart God's keys for a long and blessed life. It will renew your mind so that you will be able to receive God's promises for the renewal of your youth; and it will impart the wisdom you need to see these promises come to pass. Generally, there has been little teaching on this subject; and as a result, God's people are largely ignorant of it. As a result they are "destroyed for lack of knowledge" (Hosea 4:6), for "faith comes by hearing, and hearing by the Word of God" (Romans 10:17). In studying long life, I have been amazed to discover how much Scripture there is on this subject and how clear the Bible's teaching is in this area (see Appendix B where I have compiled a selection of Scriptures on this vital truth).

The purpose of this book is to discover from God's Word the *keys* to youth renewal and long life. What you learn will increase and enhance your days on earth. How can this be possible? First, God's Word on this subject will renew your mind, and impart *faith* into your heart so that you can *believe* and *receive* God's promises of long life. Second, it will impart the wisdom that you need to apply to your lifestyle in order to avoid the snares of death and lengthen your days. Thus you will see these promises come to pass in your life.

The first key is faith in God's promises of long life, as Jesus said, "According to *your faith* let it be to you" (Matthew 9:29). We must believe God's promises for long life, for our connection with God and His life is our faith in His Word, and that faith comes by hearing and receiving His Word (see Romans 10:17). So we must build our personal faith by studying and meditating on the long-life Scriptures until our hearts are firmly established on God's Word.

If you want to live a long and satisfying life, then the place to start is by knowing, believing, and confessing God's Word on the subject. God is faithful to His Word, so as with all of His promises, when He says, "With long life I will satisfy him" (Psalm 91:16), He means what He says. His Word is true and dependable: "all the promises of God in Him [through His death and resurrection] are Yes, and in Him Amen, to the glory [manifestation] of God through us" (2 Corinthians 1:20). If we ask: is the promise of God for me? God says: Yes!, and He wants us to add our Amen! in faith-agreement, for then He can bring the promise to manifestation in our lives, through us—through our faith.

Therefore, long life is His will for us, and it is an important part of our inheritance in Christ, which we need to know about so that we can lay hold of it and possess it by faith and thereby enjoy this wonderful blessing by having full and long lives. It is vital we know and believe God's promises in this area so that we can have full and satisfying lives, rather than seeing them cut short before we can fulfill our years. We must know God's promises on long life and be fully persuaded of it before we can embrace—believe we receive—it.

Now if God gives believers promises of long life (and He does), then surely health, healing, and long life must be His general will for us. But God's promises of longevity come with conditions, and so they are not fulfilled automatically. Now when God puts conditions on a promise, He is not trying to make it difficult for us to receive it, as if it were not really His will. No! God is not double-minded. The fact that He makes the promise proves that it is His will. Then, because it is His will, He also adds the conditions to impart to us the wisdom we need to apply to our lifestyle so that we can see the promise fulfilled in our lives. Thus He shows us what to do and what to avoid, for God knows what will shorten and what will lengthen our lives.

In conclusion, God gives us the promise to reveal His will and build up our faith to receive the promise, and He gives us the conditions for the promise to be fulfilled, so that we can walk in wisdom, doing those things that will lengthen our lives and avoiding the things that will cut our lives short and abort the fulfillment of God's promise of long life.

In this book, you will discover the *keys to long life*, which include the key of *faith* (in God's promise for long life), along with a number of other keys of *wisdom* (the skillful application of God's Word to our lives). So we will see God's promises for long and full lives, which will build up our faith. Also we will discover the conditions that we must satisfy in our lives for these promises to be fulfilled. We will see the Bible has many promises for us on this issue and much guidance for us to attain long and full lives.

Knowing and appropriating God's wonderful promises of long life is essential to completing our race and fulfilling the call of God on our lives, as well as providing a witness to the world of God's renewing and keeping power.

Study the Word of God until you can hear God say to you, "With *long life* I will satisfy you" (Psalm 91:16). When you believe His promises, you will be able to confidently say in the face of danger, disease, and death, "I shall not die [young], but [I shall] live [long], and declare the works of the Lord" (Psalm 118:17).

Chapter 1

THE IMPORTANCE OF KNOWING GOD'S WILL

When people die they share their wealth with those they love through their last will and testament, which is legally binding. The inheritance is given freely to the heirs upon death, which they can then receive through a knowledge of the will. However there is a danger that through ignorance the heirs may not claim their inheritance, and as a result they will miss out on enjoying what is theirs.

Likewise, when Jesus died on the Cross, He made full provision for us (believers) for every area of our life. Second Peter 1:3 says, "His divine power has given to us all things that pertain to life and godliness." Our inheritance in Christ is set forth clearly in His Last Will and Testament—the New Testament or Covenant, a legally binding document. By studying it with the help of the Holy Spirit, we can know what has been freely given to us in Christ through His blood:

> But as it is written, "Eye has not seen, nor ear heard, nor have entered into the heart of man the things which God has prepared for those who love Him." But God has revealed them to us through His Spirit. For the Spirit searches all things, yes, the deep things of God. For what man knows the things of a man except the spirit of the man which is in him? Even so no one knows the things of God except the Spirit of God. Now we have received, not the spirit of the world, but the Spirit who is from God, that we might know the things that have been freely given to us by God (1 Corinthians 2:9-12).

COVENANT BLESSINGS

These Covenant blessings have already been given to us. Our inheritance in Christ contains every blessing of life, which therefore includes long life. They include abundance of life both now and for all eternity:

- Ephesians 1:3: "Blessed be the God and Father of our Lord Jesus Christ, who has blessed us with *every spiritual blessing* in the heavenly places in Christ."

- John 10:10: "The thief does not come except to steal, and to kill, and to destroy. I [Jesus] have come *that they may have life*, and that they may have it more abundantly."

- 2 Peter 1:3: "His divine power has given to us all things that pertain to life and godliness...."

- Romans 8:32: "He who did not spare His own Son, but delivered Him up for us all [to die on the Cross], how shall He not with Him also *freely give us all things?*"

If God loved us so much that He did not even withhold His Son from us, would He withhold any good thing from us? Psalm 84:11 says, "No good thing will He withhold from those who walk uprightly." God is not holding back any good thing from His people, rather He freely gives us all things.

So we have a wonderful inheritance in Christ that has been released to us through the death of Christ. However if we are not diligent in studying the Scriptures which reveal the blessings and conditions of His will, then we will remain ignorant about our inheritance and as a result we will fail to receive (obtain) by faith what has been freely given to us. That is why God says in Hosea 4:6: "My people are destroyed for lack of knowledge..." (ignorance of His Word).

God does not force His blessings upon us. He gives them freely to us in the New Covenant, but we must still receive them by faith. He makes them freely available to us in Christ, but they must be received through our faith; as Jesus said, "According to your faith let it be to you" (Matthew 9:29). Now faith only begins when the will of God is known, for you cannot believe God beyond your knowledge of His will! Now *God's Word is His will!*

Therefore, in order to receive any part of your inheritance from God (such as long life), you must first study the Word in that area to *know* His will. Only then will you have the *faith* in your heart by which you can possess (receive) the promise of God. Otherwise you will not be able to lay hold of God's provision—it will remain unclaimed inheritance. So it is essential for you to hear and receive God's Word on the subject.

In Romans 10, Paul makes this process of faith very clear. Romans 10:12 says, "For there is no distinction between Jew and Greek, for the same Lord over all is rich to all who call upon Him." God has a rich inheritance that He is ready to release to us, as soon as we call on Him in faith; which means believing His promise, we come to Him and receive it.

Romans 10:13 says, "For 'whoever calls on the Name of the Lord shall be saved'" (see Joel 2:32). All who call upon the Lord and His salvation (inheritance), believing they receive it, shall have it (see Mark 11:24), for He gives it freely to us. He makes it freely available to all, but He does not force it on us. He just waits for us to believe Him and come to Him to receive it.

Romans 10:14,17 says, "How then shall they call on Him in whom they have not believed? And how shall they believe in Him of whom they have not heard? And how shall they hear without a preacher? So then faith (to receive from God) comes by hearing, and hearing by the word of God."

It is impossible to call on Him (come to Him in prayer and receive it by faith) if you don't believe His promise (Word), and it is impossible to believe it if you have never heard it! Therefore it must all start by hearing the Word (promise), which brings faith to your heart, enabling you to come to God in prayer and receive the promise (calling on His name). Then He will release the riches of your inheritance to you.

The same truth is revealed in Second Peter 1:3-4:

> *His divine power has given to us all things that pertain to life and godliness, through the knowledge of Him who called us by glory and virtue, by which have been given to us exceedingly great and precious promises, that through these you may be partakers of the divine nature....*

God has already freely given us all things needful for life, but we can only receive them (by faith) through having a knowledge of Him (His faithfulness) and His will. He gives us this knowledge through His great and precious promises that cover every area of life. Through hearing His Word concerning any area of life, we gain knowledge of His will to bless us in that area and the faith to receive that blessing. Then by faith we can partake (believe we receive) of His life.

OUR INHERITANCE

We have a wonderful inheritance: "In Him [Christ] also we have obtained an *inheritance*" (Ephesians 1:11). This became ours when we were saved and became children of God: "The Spirit Himself bears witness with our spirit that we are children of God, and if children, then heirs—heirs of God and joint heirs with Christ…" (Romans 8:16-17). This is confirmed by God's description of Paul's ministry in Acts 26:18:

> To open their eyes, in order to turn them from darkness to light, and from the power of Satan to God, that they may receive forgiveness of sins and an inheritance among them who are sanctified by faith in Me.

However it is up to us to partake of (claim) our inheritance. Colossians 1:12-13 says:

> Giving thanks to the Father who has qualified us to be *partakers of the inheritance* of the saints in the light. He has delivered us from the power of darkness and conveyed us into the kingdom of the Son of His love.

In order to enter in and possess our inheritance we must have the faith that comes from receiving the Word of God:

> So now, brethren, I commend you to God and to the word of His grace [what He has freely given to us], which is able to build you up and give you an inheritance among all those who are sanctified (Acts 20:32).

If we do not *know* the promise of God in some area of life, then it is impossible to *believe* it, and so come to God in faith and *partake* of it (believe we receive it). As a result we miss out on the blessing of God.

LONG LIFE

Long life is an important area of our inheritance in Christ and we need to *know* and *claim* the promises of long life if we want to experience and enjoy this part of our inheritance.

Imagine you bought lots of chocolates, enough for all your family and friends to enjoy. You choose to give them away as free gifts, so you tell all your family and friends, "I have paid in full for them and I freely give them to you all. They are yours. Just come to me and receive them; you can take whatever you need. They are freely available upon request." Although you have paid for and want to give the chocolates away, people still have to believe you and come to you and receive them.

Likewise with His blood, Jesus has paid in full for every blessing of our inheritance, and He has freely given it to us so that it is ours for the taking. But we still have to come to Him in faith and receive what He has freely given to us.

So He tells us the Word of His grace; the Good News that the promised blessing is ours in Christ so that faith might be imparted to our hearts. We believe His promise and come to Him in faith, believing that we receive the promised blessing.

Hebrews 4:16 says, "Let us therefore come *boldly* [with confident faith] to the throne of *grace*, that we may *obtain* [receive] mercy and find grace to help in time of need."

To obtain the blessing means that we actually *believe we receive* it from God and walk away from His throne in possession of it. This requires the boldness or confidence that only comes from knowing His promise, and from knowing that the promised blessing has already been freely given to us, is available upon request, and will be given to us, when we ask, by a God who is faithful to His Word. Thus this confidence that we can come and receive it is based on us knowing that we are coming to the throne of grace—the place where God freely and abundantly gives (releases to) us the promised blessing.

POSSESSING THE PROMISED LAND

As with any promise of God, in order to enjoy the promise of long life, we must possess it by faith. God gave us a wonderful picture of this in Israel's possessing of her Promised Land. God gave Israel a wonderful inheritance—the Promised Land—but they still had to go in and possess it by faith. Likewise we have a promised land of blessings in Christ, including long life. Just like Israel we have to possess it by believing the Word of God and fighting the fight of faith.

Even though God had given them the Land, because of their unbelief (they had not established God's Word in their hearts), they initially failed to possess it. Then when they had a second chance, God gave Joshua clear instructions for possessing the Land. He told him that the Land was their inheritance from God. He clearly described the boundaries of the Land so they knew exactly what belonged to them. He said He was giving them the Land, but they still had to go in and possess (claim) it, by putting their foot on it: "Every place that the sole of your foot will tread upon, I have given you." Therefore God told them to "go in to possess the Land which the Lord your God is giving you to possess" (see Joshua 1:2-4,6,11).

This required them 1) to have a strong faith in God's Word, and 2) to be courageous to act on it, "Be [1] strong [in faith] and [2] of good courage [to act on the Word].... Only be [1] strong [in faith] and [2] very courageous, that you may observe to do [God's Word]...do not turn from it to the right hand or to the left, that you may prosper wherever you go. ...Have I not commanded you? Be [1] strong [in faith] and [2] of good courage [to act]; do not be afraid, nor be dismayed, for the Lord your God is with you wherever you go" (Joshua 1:6-7,9).

The key to being strong enough in faith to go in and possess the promised inheritance is receiving and knowing the Word of God:

> *This Book of the Law shall not depart from your mouth, but you shall meditate in it day and night, that you may observe to do according to all that is written in it. For then you will make your way prosperous, and then you will have good success* [in possessing the inheritance] (Joshua 1:8).

Likewise we need to study God's Word so that we know our inheritance in Christ that has been freely given to us, and so we will have the faith to go in and possess (claim) it.

POINTS TO PONDER

1. When Jesus died on the Cross, He made full provision for you in every area of your life.

2. God has already freely given you all things needful for life, but you can only receive them (by faith) through having a knowledge of Him (His faithfulness) and His will.

3. The key to being strong enough in faith to go in and possess your promised inheritance is receiving and knowing the Word of God.

Chapter 2

GOD'S PROMISES FOR LONG LIFE

First of all, let us look at some of these precious promises to build our faith that God's will is for us to have long lives. Knowing God's will is the foundation for our faith. We need to establish our faith on God's promises of healing and long life *now*. Don't wait until your body is threatened before you start receiving these promises. Build up your health and immunity to sickness now by meditating on these promises.

We need to build up our faith for health and long life now by knowing, believing, and speaking out these promises. By faith we need to daily lay hold of God's provision of life and healing for our body, for I believe that Jesus said that healing is the children's bread (see Matthew 15:26), and every day we should pray, "Give us this day our daily bread" [our daily healing] (Matthew 6:11). This way we will be training ourselves so that we will be able to lay hold of God's life and healing when we really need it, and that we will be able to resist sickness and death when it comes against us.

There are many promises in the Bible that show that God's will for us is to have a long and full life. God gives us these promises, so that our faith is built up to receive this blessing from Him. He also tells us what we need to do in our life in order for these promises to be fulfilled.

PROMISES

In Exodus 23:25-26, God reveals His will for us: "You shall serve the Lord your God, and He will *bless* your bread and water. And I will take sickness away from the midst of you. ...I will fulfill the [full] number

21

of your days." His will is to bless and His blessing is health and long life. God wants us to live full lives, rather than having them be cut short.

Deuteronomy 11:18-21 says:

> *Therefore you shall lay up these words of mine in your heart and in your soul, and bind them as a sign on your hand, and they shall be as frontlets between your eyes. You shall teach them to your children, speaking of them when you sit in your house, when you walk by the way, when you lie down, and when you rise up. And you shall write them on the doorposts of your house and on your gates, that your days and the days of your children may be multiplied in the land of which the Lord swore to your fathers to give them, like the days of the heavens above the earth.*

We see that God's best for His people is both quantity and quality of life. He wants to multiply our days in the earth and make them like days of heaven on earth—days of love, joy, and peace.

Clearly it must be God's will for us to have long life! Deuteronomy 30:19-20 says:

> *I call heaven and earth as witnesses today against you, that I have set before you life and death, blessing and cursing; therefore choose life, that both you and your descendants may live; that you may love the Lord your God, that you may obey His voice, and that you may cling to Him, for* **He** *is your life and the length of your days....*

God wants us to choose life, and He makes that life available to us so that we can have it, if we make the right decision to choose life. This offer of life clearly includes length of days, proving that long life is His will for us. He also tells us how to make the right choice and receive the long life that He offers.

He is our life and the length of our days, so by drawing close to Him we draw close to the Source of our life. By *loving* Him and *clinging* to Him in faith, we will draw upon His life, which will lengthen our days. As we trust Him and His promises of life, He is able to impart that life to us.

> *For the Lord God is a sun* [radiating health to us] *and shield* [protecting us from sickness]; *the Lord will give grace and*

glory; no good thing [including long life] *will He withhold from those who walk uprightly. O Lord of hosts, blessed is the man who trusts in You!* (Psalm 84:11-12)

Bless the Lord, O my soul, and forget not all His benefits: Who forgives all your iniquities, Who heals all your diseases, Who redeems your life from destruction, Who crowns you with lovingkindness and tender mercies, Who satisfies your mouth with good things, so that your youth is renewed like the eagle's (Psalm 103:2-5).

God's benefits include forgiveness from all sins, healing from all diseases, deliverance from destruction (early death) and the renewal of our youth (long life). We are to remember ("forget not") all these benefits promised in the Word, by acknowledging them and thanking God for them. Thus we are to take God's promises of healing and long life upon our lips and thank God for these promised blessings, saying, "Thank You, Lord, for forgiving all my sins, for healing all my sicknesses, and for renewing my youth like the eagle."

Proverbs 3:1-2 says, "My son, forget not my law, but let your heart keep my commands; for length of days and long life and peace shall they add to you." This speaks of both quality and quantity of life. Peace (*shalom*) describes good, fruitful days of blessing and wholeness. Length of days and long life speaks of many days. So this tells us that God wants us to have full, satisfying and long lives, which is possible if we pay attention to His Word.

*Happy is the man who finds wisdom, and the man who gains understanding; for her proceeds are better than the profits of silver, and her gain than fine gold. She is more precious than rubies, and all the things you may desire cannot compare with her. Length of days is in her right hand, in her left hand riches and honor. Her ways are ways of pleasantness, and all her paths are peace. She is a **tree of life** to those who take hold of her, and happy are all who retain her* (Proverbs 3:13-18).

God's wisdom is found in His Word. Here God is motivating us to seek and find His wisdom by promising us that if we find her, and take hold of her and keep her, she will bring life and length of days to us. So again we see His will for us is long life:

- Proverbs 4:10: "Hear, my son, and receive my sayings, and [as a result] the years of your life will be many." God wants us to have many years of life, through receiving His Word.

- Proverbs 9:10-11: "The fear of the Lord [respect and reverence for His authority] is the beginning of wisdom, and knowledge of the Holy One is understanding. For by me [wisdom] your days will be multiplied, and years of life will be added to you." God wants you to lengthen your life by receiving His wisdom, which will begin to happen when you humble yourself before God and His Word.

- Proverbs 10:27: "The fear of the Lord prolongs days, but the years of the wicked will be shortened." Sin will always bring death, but God wants you to prolong your days.

- 1 Kings 3:14: "If you walk in My ways, to keep My statutes and My commandments ...then I will lengthen your days." Here God said to Solomon, as He says to us, "If you walk in My ways, I will lengthen your days." God wants us to live long and gives us the promise of long life, but it is conditional on us walking with Him. If we walk close to the Source of life, His life will rub off on us.

- Exodus 20:12: "Honor your father and your mother, that your days may be long upon the land which the Lord your God is giving you." This is so important, that God made this one of the Ten Commandments that He wrote with His own finger in stone! It is the first Commandment with a promise. He promises us that if we respect and honor our parents, our days will be long upon the earth.

- Deuteronomy 5:16: "Honor your father and your mother, as the Lord your God has commanded you, that your days may be long, and that it may be well with you in the land which the Lord your God is giving you." Forty years later God repeated and enhanced the promise of Exodus 20:12 of long life. Now He promises both quantity and quality of life. Not only will our days on earth be long (many days), but they will also be good days ("it will be well with you").

- Psalm 34:12-13: "Who is the man who desires life, and loves many days, that he may see good? Keep your tongue from evil, and your lips from speaking deceit." Here God encourages our desire to see many good days, by giving us a major key to attaining this: keeping our tongues from speaking evil. He promises that if we will guard our tongues, we will enjoy a long life and see many good days.

My favorite is from Psalm 91, which is full of promises about how God will preserve and protect our lives if we will trust in Him. It concludes with God speaking directly in verses 14-16:

Because he has set his love on Me, I will deliver him; I will set him on high, because he has known My name. He shall call upon Me, and I will answer him; I will be with him in trouble; I will deliver him and honor him. With long life I will satisfy him and show [manifest to] *him My salvation* [preservation from death].

In Psalm 91:16, God's promise is for the person who lives in the secret place of the Almighty, under the shadow of His wings: "With long life I will I satisfy him." To satisfy means to be full as in after a good meal. God wants us to be satisfied, for us to go through a full life cycle and for it not to be cut short. "I give them life, long and full, and show them how I can save" (Jerusalem Bible). That is what God wants to do for us. His best will for us is to be satisfied, so if we are not satisfied with 70 years, then we can go on to 80, 90, 100, even 120 until we are satisfied!

Long life means many days, and the fact that we will be satisfied with them means that they will also be good days, where we maintain our basic health and soundness of mind. So this is a promise of both quantity and quality of life. Of course we cannot live forever in this mortal body, but we can live a life that is full of days, rather than seeing it cut short.

The life story of Kenneth Hagin is very instructive for us. He was healed as 17-year-old from a terminal blood disease and paralysis by acting on Mark 11:24: "Therefore I say to you, whatever things you ask [including healing], when you pray, believe that you receive them, and you will have them."

Having been bed-bound for some time, after receiving his healing Hagin was now able to get up and go to breakfast. However, naturally he was still weak, so after breakfast he went back to his room to rest. Soon afterward he heard a deep supernatural audible voice come to his mind saying, "What is your life? It is even a vapor that appears for a little while and then vanishes (see James 4:14). You have been healed but everyone is appointed once to die (see Hebrews 9:27) and today your appointed time has come. You shall surely die and not live" (see Isaiah 38:1). Hagin thought it must be God speaking and quoting Scripture! So, he sat down waiting for death. (Note that something supernatural like this is not necessarily God. The devil can quote Scripture, but it will be twisted and taken out of context and misapplied.)

Then, inside, from his spirit, came bubbling up the words: "With long life will I satisfy him and show him My salvation." He did not even know that was in the Bible. Then the other voice reasserted itself saying the same thing. Then again came bubbling up on the inside: "With long life will I satisfy him and show him My salvation."

Then he heard the deep voice for a third time. And for a third time he heard the inner voice say, "With long life will I satisfy him and show him My salvation." Then Hagin asked, "Who said that?" The inner voice said, "The 91st Psalm." He looked it up and read: "with long life will I satisfy him." He thought, "Well, I am only 17; I am not satisfied yet. The Bible promises I will be satisfied with a long life." But the other voice came back saying, "Yes, but that promise was for the Jews, not for the Church. It was an Old Testament blessing."

So Hagin decided to check all the cross references to see if this promise is repeated in the New Testament for then he could be sure that it applied to him—and us. He soon found Ephesians 6:2-3: "Honor your father and mother (the first commandment with promise): That it may be well with you, and you may live long on the earth" (quoting from Exodus 20:12 and Deuteronomy 5:16). Here God makes it clear that He wants us to have long life with many good days. Clearly this promise is in the New Testament and so it still applies to us today.

Hagin also found First Peter 3:9-10 in the New Testament: "You were called to this, that you may inherit a blessing. For "He who would love life and see (many) good days, let him refrain his tongue from evil..." (from Psalm 34:12-16). We (in the New Covenant) are called to inherit a blessing. What blessing? The blessing of many good days! He also realized that God does not change and that we now we have a New and better Covenant than the Old Covenant that Israel was under. Hebrews 8:6 says, "He [Jesus] is also the Mediator of a better covenant, which was established on better promises." So if the promise of long life was in the Old Covenant, then surely it applies to us also now; otherwise, the New Covenant would be inferior to the Old Covenant.

Realizing this, Kenneth Hagin knew the first voice was satan impersonating God, trying to make him give up and passively accept sickness and death as God's will. So he stood up and declared out loud, "Devil, I'm not going to die today, I'm not going to die tomorrow, I'm not going to die next week, I'm not going to die next year, I'm not going to die in five years, I'm not going to die in ten years, I'm not going to die in twenty years, I'm not going to die in thirty, forty, or even fifty years. I will be satisfied with a long life." And it came to pass that he did live a long and fruitful life before going on to be with the Lord. Likewise we need to establish our faith now to live in God's promises of long life, as this 17-year-old did.

The promises of long life are not just in the Old Testament, they are reaffirmed in the New Testament in Ephesians 6:2-3 and First Peter 3:9-10. This is confirmed in John 10:10 where Jesus said that He came to give us abundant life, which must include a long and full life on earth as well as eternal life in heaven. Moreover, Second Corinthians 1:20 says, "All the promises of God [including long life] in Him [Christ] are Yes, and in Him [we say the] Amen, to the glory [manifestation] of God through us [through our faith]." Through the blood of Jesus, God confirms to us that every promise is ours in Christ. But we must know and receive (embrace) the promise for ourselves, adding our Amen by confessing the promise as true for us. Then it will surely come to pass to the glory of God through us.

Long life is God's will for us. God has promised it to us in the New Covenant in Christ. So let us believe and receive these promises now and establish our faith in God now for a long and blessed life. We need to know these promises so well that no one could ever talk us out of believing them.

We have seen that an abundant and long life is God's will for us (see John 10:10), so much so that Jesus took the curse of an early death for us so that we could have the blessing of long and full lives (see Galatians 3:13-14)! Therefore, if we seek to fulfill God's will and best for our lives, we need to believe and pray for His will to be done in our lives, which includes living a long life. As we trust God daily for His abundant life to sustain us in good health, soundness of mind, and strength of body throughout a long and full life, we will glorify God and be a witness to His loving care and renewing power. Thus others will be drawn to Him through us.

POINTS TO PONDER

1. Build up your faith for health and long life now by knowing, believing, and speaking out His promises—by faith, daily lay hold of God's provision of life and healing for your body, mind and spirit.

2. God promises that if you will guard your tongue, you will enjoy a long life and see many good days.

3. Believe and receive God's promises for a long and blessed life—know and speak these promises so well that no one could ever talk you out of believing them.

Chapter 3

IS THERE AN APPOINTED TIME TO DIE?

Is the length of our life preordained? In that encounter with Kenneth Hagin, satan misquoted Hebrews 9:27 which says, "It is appointed for men to die once, but after this the judgment." This does *not* say there is an appointed time to die as if God has fixed the day of our death and so there is nothing we can do about it. What it actually says is that each person has one life on earth and one death after which each will stand before God to be judged. This verse proves that reincarnation is a lie. Yes, we have an appointment with death (if the Lord does not return first in the Rapture), and we also have an appointment with judgment (for we shall all stand before the Lord to give an account of how we have lived our lives), but God has not appointed (fixed) the time of our death. To a great extent, that time is up to us, for God respects our free will. So we are appointed to die one day, but we don't have an appointed (pre-ordained) time to die. To think otherwise would be fatalism, which the Bible does not teach.

Now God knows all things, so He knows the end from the beginning, He knows the choices we will make, and He knows the ultimate length of our lives: "Your eyes saw my substance, being yet unformed. And in Your book they all were written, the days fashioned for me, when as yet there were none of them" (Psalm 139:16). However, God does not infringe our free will by predetermining exactly when we will die, but rather He gives us freedom to affect the length of our lives through our choices.

Does not Ecclesiastes 3:1-2 say there is a time to die? "To everything there is a season, a time for every purpose under heaven: a time to be born, and a time to die; a time to plant, and a time to pluck what is planted." This verse is saying there is a right or proper time to die. There is a rhythm to life on earth, there are cycles of life that every living thing goes through. Here the human life span is compared to a plant from its planting (birth) to its plucking (death). There is a proper season and time to die, just as there is a proper time to harvest a crop. What is that time? It is when it has reached a full ripe age or maturity. You do not harvest a crop when it has just begun to spring up. You would be harvesting it before its proper time. Likewise the time to die is at a full age, after a fully developed life.

As Job 5:26 says, "You shall come to your grave at a full age, as a sheaf of grain ripens in its [proper] season." The season to die is at a full age. We do not harvest a crop when it is half grown. Mid-life is not your time to die!

SIN AND FOOLISHNESS

There are things you do that shorten and lengthen your life. The Bible is clear that when you die is not all up to God. Ecclesiastes 7:17 says, "Do not be overly [1] wicked, nor be [2] foolish: why should you die before your [proper] time?" [full age]. Here we are told two ways we can shorten our time on earth so that we die before the full life span God wants us to enjoy.

1. *Being wicked will shorten our lives.* Sin will shorten your life, for "the wages of sin is death" (Romans 6:23). If you put your work and effort into a sinful lifestyle, you will receive its wages—death. That is, death will come to you sooner than it should. Psalm 55:23 says, "bloodthirsty and deceitful men shall not live out half their days; but I will trust in You" [for a long life]. And Proverbs 13:3 says, "He who guards his mouth [from speaking evil and unbelief] preserves [protects] his life, but he who opens wide his lips shall have destruction." And it has already been mentioned that Ephesians 6:2-3 (from Exodus 20:12 and Deuteronomy 5:16) says, "'Honor your father and mother,' which is the first commandment with promise: 'that it may be well with you and you may live long on the earth.'" If we dishonor our parents, then it is

30

impossible for it to go well with us and for us to live long on the earth. In other words, our life will be cut short.

Psalm 34:12-13 (also 1 Peter 3:9-10) tells us, "Who is the man who desires life, and loves many days, that he may see good? Keep your tongue from evil, and your lips from speaking deceit." Clearly if we fail to keep our tongue from speaking evil, we will disqualify ourselves from seeing the promise fulfilled. Again we see the length of our life depends on our choices.

2. Being foolish will also shorten our lives. There are also foolish things that we can do that may not be sinful, but they will also shorten our lives. If we do not eat properly or take care of our bodies in other ways, we will pay a price. If we go out into the cold and wet not properly dressed, that is foolish. If we do not listen to the advice of those with more experience and take unnecessary risks, that may not necessarily be sinful, but it certainly is foolish, and foolishness can seriously shorten our lives.

But praise God, we can also add years to our life on earth!

KEEP GOD'S WORD

Sin and foolishness will take time off our lives, but God's Word in us will add and even multiply days to our lives. God's Word in us will increase the number of our days.

> *My son, do not forget my law, but let your heart keep my commands; for length of days and long life and peace they [God's words] will add to you* (Proverbs 3:1-2).

> *My son, receive my sayings, and* [as a result] *the years of your life will be many* (Proverbs 4:10).

In Deuteronomy 11:18-21 God promises increased quantity and quality of life, if we will put His Word first:

> *You shall lay up these words of mine in your heart and in your soul, and bind them as a sign on your hand, and they shall be as frontlets between your eyes. You shall teach them to your children, speaking of them when you sit in your house, when you walk by the way, when you lie down, and when you rise up. And you shall write them on the doorposts of your house and on your*

gates, that your days and the days of your children may be multiplied in the land of which the Lord swore to your fathers to give them, like the days of the heavens above the earth.

If we keep God's Word ever before us, it will multiply and enrich our days on earth.

Proverbs 9:11 says, "By me [wisdom] your days shall be multiplied, and years of life will be added to you." God's wisdom is in His Word, so as we receive the wisdom of His Word into our hearts, that wisdom will cause our days to be multiplied and our years to be increased. If we sow our attention to God's Word, we will reap God's (eternal, reenergizing) life, both in this life and in eternity—but if we sow to the flesh, we shall reap death and destruction:

Do not be deceived, God is not mocked; for whatever a man sows, that he will also reap. For he who sows to his flesh will of the flesh reap corruption, but he who sows to the Spirit will of the Spirit reap everlasting life (Galatians 6:7-8).

Romans 8:6 says, "For to be carnally minded is death, but *to be spiritually minded is life and peace.*" If we sow our time into the Word of God, then we will surely reap in our earthly life more time and blessing. If we will give our time to God's Word, it will give that time back to us, multiplied, in a longer life of blessed days!

Matthew 6:33 says, "Seek first the kingdom of God and His righteousness, and all these things [of this life, including days] shall be added to you" [length of life added to us]. If you are tempted to think, "I don't have time for the Word of God," you should remember that any time you invest in the Word will be multiplied back to you. But if you live without the Word, your life will be shortened. So if you are wise, the first priority for the use of your time will be to put it into the Word.

Happy is the man who finds wisdom, and the man who gains understanding [from God's Word]; for her proceeds are better than the profits of silver, and her gain than fine gold. She is more precious than rubies, and all the things you may desire cannot compare with her. Length of days is in her right hand. In her left hand is riches and honor. Her ways are ways of pleasantness, and all her paths are peace. She is a tree [source] of life to those who take hold of her, and happy are all who retain her (Proverbs 3:13-18).

As we study God's Word, we will receive God's wisdom imparted into our hearts. This wisdom is our most valuable asset, continually giving to us precious proceeds and profits, such as health and long life. She carries with her length of days, so when we lay hold of her and keep her close to our hearts, we will also receive what she brings with her. Thus when we receive God's Word into our hearts, it will then produce byproducts in our lives, which include long life.

LIVE RIGHT AND SERVE GOD

We will lengthen our lives by living right and serving God. If we walk in integrity and righteousness in our treatment of others, our days (life) will be lengthened.

> *You shall have a perfect and just weight, a perfect and just measure, that your days may be lengthened in the land which the Lord your God is giving you* (Deuteronomy 25:15).

> *A ruler who lacks understanding is a great oppressor, but he who hates covetousness will prolong his days* (Proverbs 28:16).

God promises us as He promised Solomon in First Kings 3:14: "If you walk in My ways, to keep My statutes and My commandments… then I will lengthen your days." And Exodus 23:25-26 says, "You shall serve the Lord your God, and He will bless your bread and water. And I will take sickness away from the midst of you. I will fulfill the [full] number of your days" [your full life span].

As mentioned previously, there are many promises of God for long life, revealing the fact that it is God's general will for us. However these promises are conditional on what we believe and do. Their fulfillment depends on us, therefore the length of our lives is not preordained—we can increase it or decrease it.

This is also revealed in the classic long-life Scripture in Psalm 91:

> *Because he has set his love upon Me, therefore I will deliver him; I will set him on high, because he has known My name. He shall call upon Me, and I will answer him; I will be with him in*

trouble; I will deliver him and honor him. **With long life I will satisfy him, and show him My salvation** *(Psalm 91:14-16).*

The promise of long life is only for the person who sets his love upon God. Literally, this means he clings to God in faith and humble dependence. As he abides under the shadow of the Almighty and clings to God (the Source of life), so God's life is imparted to him and God is able to fulfill His promise to him of long life. Clearly the length of his life depends on his fellowship with God and faith in God. By loving and trusting God, the man in Psalm 91 received a long, satisfying life from God, whereas the outcome would have been quite different if he had not lived his life that way.

CHOOSE LIFE!

So we have a choice to either shorten our life or lengthen it. Proverbs 10:27 says, "The fear of the Lord prolongs days, but the years of the wicked will be shortened." God gives us the choice of life or death, blessing or cursing—and He wants us to choose life and blessing.

> *I call heaven and earth as witnesses today against you, that I have set before you life and death, blessing and cursing; therefore choose life that both you and your descendants may live; that you may love the Lord your God, that you may obey His voice, and that you may cling to Him, for He is your life and the length of your days...* (Deuteronomy 30:19-20).

Notice life and blessing is set over against death and cursing. Life in all its forms (physical and spiritual) is a blessing. Death in all its forms (physical and spiritual) is the curse. God is life, He is our life, so being connected to God brings the blessing of life, but separation from Him results in the curse of death. He wants us to choose life; and the way we choose life is to choose Him for *He is life.* The blessing of life that God promises here to those who love Him clearly includes length of days: "for He is your life and the length of your days." Therefore long life is a blessing from God, but it is our choice whether to receive it. He is the Source of life, so as we cling to Him, He will add life and length of days to us.

Declare with the Psalmist, "I shall not die [young], but live [long], and declare the works of the Lord" (Psalm 118:17).

POINTS TO PONDER

1. God does not infringe on your free will by predetermining exactly when you will die, but rather He gives you freedom to affect the length of your life through your choices.

2. If you give your time to God's Word, He will give that time back to you, multiplied, in a longer life of blessed days!

3. As you abide under the shadow of the Almighty and cling to God (the Source of life), so God's life is imparted to you and God will fulfill His promise to you of long life.

Chapter 4

THE RENEWAL OF OUR YOUTH, PART I

We have seen that part of our inheritance in Christ (God's will for us) is to have abundant life, which includes a good and long life loving and serving the Lord, as well as eternal life and glory. Psalm 91:16 says of the person who puts all his trust in the Lord: "With long life I will satisfy Him and show him My salvation." Connected to God's promises of long life are His promises of youth renewal; for to live long, we surely need our youth to be renewed. We will see many exciting examples of this in the lives of the Bible heroes.

Psalm 103:1-5 says that this was not just for them, but for all believers. These verses tell us about the benefits of the Lord to us:

> Bless the Lord, O my soul; and all that is within me, bless His holy name! Bless the Lord O my soul, and forget not [remember] all His benefits:
>
> [1] Who forgives all your iniquities [this is for all],
>
> [2] Who heals all your diseases [this is for all],
>
> [3] Who redeems your life from destruction [the curse],
>
> [4] Who crowns you with lovingkindness and tender mercies,
>
> [5] Who satisfies your mouth with good things, so that your youth is renewed like the eagle's.

Youth renewal is a benefit of God that is available for all believers, and we should believe for it and thank and bless God for it, saying:

"Bless the Lord, He renews my youth." Psalm 103 tells us that we should *remember to receive and thank* (bless) God for all of His gracious benefits to us. We should not forget or neglect to receive and thank God for any of His benefits. One of these vital benefits is the renewal of our youth. In order to enjoy long life, we must know how to receive the renewing of our youth, life, and strength.

Eagles have long lives, perhaps greater than any other bird, even up to 100 years. Often an eagle can look like it is old, but then it molts and its feathers are renewed so that it seems to become young again—its youth and strength are renewed. It gets a new lease of life and once again it is able to stretch its mighty wings and rise up high on the winds.

When we feel as if we are beginning to wind down, getting older and more tired, and forgetting things more often, God wants to provide us a renewal of youth. He wants to give us a new lease of life to reenergize us into long life. Now there is a natural aging process at work, but God can still infuse His life and strength into our bodies and minds so that we can rise up again with fresh wings as an eagle with renewed feathers, and soar again as before:

> *Have you not known? Have you not heard? The everlasting God, the Lord, the Creator of the ends of the earth, neither faints nor is weary. His understanding is unsearchable. **He gives power to the weak,** and **to those who have no might He increases strength.** Even the youths shall faint and be weary, and the young men shall utterly fall. But those who wait on* [entwine themselves with] *the Lord shall renew* [exchange] *their strength* [youth]; *they shall mount* [rise] *up with wings like eagles, they shall run and not be weary, they shall walk and not faint* [their youth renewed] (Isaiah 40:28-31).

The key is to come to God in our weakness and wait upon Him. The word *wait* means entwine, and it pictures two ropes wrapped around each other so that the smaller and weaker rope receives strength from the larger, stronger rope. We are to draw near to God and wrap ourselves around Him so that His strength comes into us and fills our weakness. In this way our strength will be renewed by His strength. The word *renewed* is literally "exchanged", so we exchange our weakness with His strength. So if we come to God in prayer and draw upon

His strength, He will renew our strength, life, and youth, overcoming our tiredness and weakness so that we will not become weary or faint.

BIBLE HEROES

Let us look at how the Bible heroes discovered this secret. Apostle Paul learned how to draw new life and strength from God by faith when he was feeling weak and tired. When he was at the end of his strength, God told Paul that His grace was sufficient for him in his weakness. This means that God's renewing and rejuvenating life and strength is freely available to us as a free gift of grace, and we can receive it at any time. Moreover, God taught Paul to welcome these times of conscious weakness as opportunities to deepen his dependence on God and lay hold of His life and power all the more, for it is only when we are aware of our weakness and need for God's help that we call out to God from the depths of our hearts for His life to fill and renew us. As a result, the more we are aware of our weakness, the more we can know His power resting upon us, if we turn to Him in our weakness, trusting Him to renew, refill, and recharge us.

> He said to me, "My grace is sufficient for you, for My strength is made perfect in [your] weakness." Therefore most gladly I will rather boast in my infirmities [situations that make me aware of my weakness], that the power of Christ may rest upon me. Therefore I take pleasure in infirmities [weaknesses], in reproaches, in needs, in persecutions, in distresses, for Christ's sake. For when I am weak [in myself], then I am strong" [through the strength the Lord supplies] (2 Corinthians 12:9-10).

Thus as we get older, we need to increasingly learn to depend upon His power to renew our strength and vitality, so we receive His life into our minds and bodies. In this way we will maintain active, healthy minds and bodies into old age. However, we need to start believing for God to renew our youth in this way, even when we are relatively young.

Paul saw every test, hardship, and setback as an opportunity to believe God and experience more of His power and answered prayer so that God would be glorified through him. There is no testimony without a test! In Second Corinthians 12:9-10 Paul claimed that God's grace is sufficient for any infirmity (weakness). He surely proved this to be true in his own life, for he faced all kinds of attacks, trials, and persecutions, both physical and mental, which often brought him to the end of his strength. In fact in chapter 11 of Second Corinthians, he gave a detailed list of the kind of infirmities he had to face, and in which he found the grace (strength) of God sufficient to see him through and to revive and restore him in spirit, soul, and body:

> *I am more: in labors more abundant, in stripes above measure, in prisons more frequently, in deaths often. From the Jews five times I received forty stripes minus one. Three times I was **beaten** with rods; once I was **stoned**; three times I was **shipwrecked**; a night and a day I have been in the deep; in journeys often, in perils of waters, in perils of robbers, in perils of my own countrymen, in perils of the Gentiles, in perils in the city, in perils in the wilderness, in perils in the sea, in perils among false brethren; in weariness and toil, in sleeplessness often, in hunger and thirst, in fastings often, in cold and nakedness—besides the other things, what comes upon me daily: my deep concern for all the churches. Who is weak, and I am not weak?...* (2 Corinthians 11:23-29)

Taking Second Corinthians 12:9-10 in context, we can see that these were the kind of infirmities that Paul was talking about, and which he overcame through trusting in the sufficiency of God's grace, even as he felt totally weak in himself. This encourages us, because whatever we are likely to face is nothing compared to what he faced. So if he found God's grace sufficient in these extreme trials, surely we will too!

Notice that the infirmities that Paul went through were often life-threatening situations, in which Paul had to stand in faith to receive God's grace to save and preserve his life so that he could fulfill his ministry. He had to believe in God's power to revive and restore him again afterward. He often came to the edge of death, and had to believe in God's resurrection power to work in his body to overcome death and keep him alive, and then to renew his strength and vitality (youth) again so that he could continue with his mission:

> *We do not want you to be ignorant, brethren, of our trouble which came to us in Asia: that we were burdened beyond measure, above strength, so that we despaired even of life. Yes, we had the sentence of death in ourselves, that we should not trust*

in ourselves, but in God who raises the dead [by His resurrection power in us], who delivered us from so great a death, and does deliver us; in whom we trust that He will still deliver us (2 Corinthians 1:8-10).

… that I may know Him and the power of His resurrection, and the fellowship of His sufferings, being conformed to His death (Philippians 3:10).

There is an aging process at work that increasingly makes us aware of our weakness, but in our weakness we can lay hold of God's strength and life for our body and mind, to receive a renewing of our youth, and to overcome the power of death.

In fact, it is the weakness (need) we feel (whether from a trial or from the aging process) that should stimulate us to turn to God to draw upon and receive His life-giving grace. Thus our weakness can be the very springboard for us to receive the strength, life, and power of the Lord. Awareness of our weakness should cause us to transfer our trust from ourselves to God who raises the dead, and so is able to deliver us from the power of death and revive and renew us again. Paul often came close to death, but through faith was able to tap into God's life-giving resurrection power for his body and soul, so he could continue his ministry of declaring God's Word.

As death approached, I can hear him confessing, "I shall not die, but live, and declare the works of the Lord" (Psalm 118:17). The attacks Paul faced meant that had he not been continually believing God for *life*, death would have taken him too soon, but again and again he found God's renewing grace was available and sufficient for him to overcome death.

We are not called to be strong in our own strength, but to be strong in the strength (power) of the Lord by faith: "be strong in the Lord and in the power of His might" (Ephesians 6:10). If God commands us to be strengthened by His mighty power so that we are filled with His strength and life, then He must make it freely available for us to receive!

Paul describes his experience again in Second Corinthians 4:7-12:

We have this treasure in earthen vessels [weakness], that the excellence of the power may be of God and not of us. We are hard-pressed on every side, yet not crushed; we are perplexed, but not in despair; persecuted, but not forsaken; struck down,

*but not destroyed—always carrying about in the body the dying
of the Lord Jesus, that the life of Jesus also may be manifested
in our body. For we who live are always delivered to death for
Jesus' sake, that the life of Jesus also may be manifested in our
mortal flesh. So then death is working in us, but life in you.*

When the spirit of death pressed in upon Paul, he was able to receive
the life of Jesus manifested in his body to push back the power of death,
until his mission was fulfilled. Paul's intention in describing his sufferings and experiences of God's renewing grace for his body and soul was
to encourage us to receive the same grace (life) from God. Let's now see
where Paul expressly tells us it is available to us all.

In First Corinthians 15:57, Paul gives thanks to God for giving us
this present victory over death: "Thanks be to God who gives us the
victory [over death] through our Lord Jesus Christ." The whole chapter is about our victory over physical death through Christ, so Paul is
talking about God giving us victory over physical death. Of course this
will ultimately be fulfilled at the resurrection of the body. But notice
Paul does not say thanks be to God who *will give* us the victory, but
rather he says, "Thanks be to God who *gives* us the victory" [NOW].

Paul thanks God for giving his body resurrection life so that he can
overcome the power of death and fulfill his mission. This verse also
gives the key to how to lay hold of Christ's resurrection life for our bodies. Paul 1) believed and received the promise of victory over death
through the resurrection life of Christ, and 2) he confessed it with his
lips, thanking God for it: *"Thanks be to God, who gives us* [now, in this
life] *the victory* [over physical death] *through* [the resurrection life of]
our Lord Jesus Christ."

Paul believed that through the resurrection of Jesus Christ, God
gives us the victory over the power of death in this life. He did not just
believe it, he proclaimed it, expressing his faith by giving thanks to
God for this victory over death. He thanks God for releasing resurrection life to his body, enabling him to overcome the power of death and
fulfill his mission. Likewise, by faith we must resist the spirit of death,
and trust God's promise to impart Christ's resurrection life to our body
now, and then like Paul, *give thanks* to God in confident faith that He is
doing it, saying, "Thanks be to God who gives me the victory over
death through Christ."

Our *declarations* of faith through *confession* of the promise and through *thanksgiving* that He is doing it now, release our faith and the resurrection power of God to work within us to overcome death and renew our youth. Say with faith, "Thanks be to God who *gives me the victory* over death through my Lord Jesus Christ."

Romans 8:11 is a wonderful promise that we can claim in order to receive His resurrection life into our mortal bodies:

> *If the* [same] *Spirit of Him* [God, the Father] *who raised Jesus from the dead dwells in you,* [then] *He* [God] *who raised Christ from the dead, will* [certainly] *also give life to your mortal bodies through His Spirit who dwells in you.*

The same Holy Spirit who imparted life to the body of Jesus, and raised Him from death to life, totally overcoming the power of death upon Him, now *lives* and *abides* in us, and is ready, willing, and able to also give life to our bodies! As the Spirit of God reversed death in the body of Jesus, so He can do it for us, by giving (imparting) life to our bodies. He *will* do it, not might do it, if we ask (trust) Him!

Now some say this verse in Romans 8 only applies to the resurrection of our bodies at the last day, but I believe the emphasis of the verse is on our life now—what the indwelling Spirit will do for us *now*. It describes the Spirit living in us, as we live in our mortal (death-doomed) bodies on the earth, and giving our bodies life. It promises that God will give life to our *mortal* bodies, not to our dead bodies. Moreover the context confirms that Paul is talking about the believers' Spirit-filled lives now.

The Spirit is our Helper, and is ready, willing, and able to impart God's resurrection life to our bodies. If we believe God's promise and call on Him in faith to release this life, strength, and healing power into our bodies, then we will receive a renewal of life, strength, and health by His Spirit. We need to believe Romans 8:11 and learn how to tap into that life of the Spirit that raised Christ from death.

There is a story about Kathryn Kuhlman, who was famous for her big miracle-healing services. Oral Roberts saw that she was full of life after ministering, and asked what her secret was, because he was often exhausted after praying for so many people. Her secret was that she had learned to stand on Romans 8:11 and receive by faith the life-giving ministry of the Holy Spirit for her mortal body.

Confess: "The same Spirit of Him who raised Jesus Christ from the dead dwells in me, and He shall also quicken and give life to my mortal body by His Spirit who lives in me. Thank You, Lord, for giving me that life now."

The same mighty resurrection power that raised Jesus from death is now freely available to us who believe, through His Spirit within us, and it is able to give life to our bodies:

> *the exceeding greatness of His power toward* [available to] *us who believe* [is] *according to the working of His mighty power which He worked in Christ when He raised Him from the dead and seated Him at His right hand in the heavenly places, far above all principality and power and might and dominion, and every name that is named...* (Ephesians 1:19-21).

We should pray for a revelation of this power so we can tap into it by faith (see Ephesians 1:11-18). God is "able to do exceedingly abundantly above all we ask or think, according to the [His] power that works within us" (Ephesians 3:20). God wants us (spirit, soul, and body) to be strengthened with might by His glorious power (see Colossians 1:11). As we continually draw on God's renewing and healing power and so fulfill our years in health and long life, our lives will be a witness and demonstration of His resurrection power.

YOUTH RENEWAL FOR
ABRAHAM, SARAH, AND REBEKAH

Psalm 103:5 tells us one of God's benefits to us that we should remember to thank Him for is the *renewal of our youth*. God did this for Sarah and for Abraham. In Genesis 12, soon after entering Canaan (when Abraham was 75 and Sarah 66), there was a famine in the land, so Abraham took his family to live in Egypt. Sarah was in her late 60s, but her appearance was so impressive that Abraham felt he had to protect himself against the consequences:

> *And it came to pass, when he was close to entering Egypt that he said to Sarai his wife, "Indeed I know that you are a woman of beautiful countenance. Therefore it will happen when the Egyptians see you, that they will say, 'This is his wife'; and they will*

*kill me, but they will let you live. Please say you are my sister,
that it may be well with me for your sake and that I may live because of you"* (Genesis 12:11-13).

Abraham felt Sarah would be in such demand that they would kill
him to have her. Now it seems impossible that a woman close to 70
could have this affect even if she was exceptionally beautiful! The
only explanation is that she had received a supernatural renewing of
her youth!

As we read on, we find that Abraham's assessment of her desirability was accurate: "So it was, when Abram came into Egypt, that the
Egyptians saw the woman, that she was very beautiful. The princes of
Pharaoh also saw her and commended her to Pharaoh. And the woman
was taken to Pharaoh's house" (Genesis 12:14-15). Now the Pharaoh
had the pick of the most beautiful women in the land and even had his
princes on the lookout for them. So as soon as Sarah (66-70 years old!)
entered the land she was spotted and brought to Pharaoh, who fell for
her: "He treated Abram well for her sake. He had sheep, oxen, male
donkeys, male and female servants, female donkeys, and camels" (v16).
He even said to Abram: "I might have taken her as my wife" (v19). *God
had surely renewed her youth!*

Rebekah received the same renewal of youth as Sarah. Isaac was
forty when they married (see Genesis 25:20), so let us assume she was
twenty (thus twenty years younger). They had children twenty years
later when Isaac was sixty (v26), so she was then about forty. Fifteen
years later Abraham died when Isaac was 75 (see Genesis 21:5; 25:7).
The events of Genesis 26 took place after Abraham had died (see 25:11
and 26:1-5), and after the two boys had grown up into men (see Genesis 25:29-33). So Isaac would have been about 80, and Rebekah was
about 60 years old.

Genesis 26:1 says, "There was a famine in the land, besides the first
famine that was in the days of Abraham. And Isaac went to Abimelech
king of the Philistines, in Gerar." But 60-year-old Rebekah caused a
stir among the men in the land, so much so that Isaac felt they would
kill to have her!: "And the men of the place asked about his wife. And
he said, 'She is my sister'; for he was afraid to say, 'She is my wife,' because he thought, 'lest the men of the place kill me for Rebekah, because she is beautiful to behold'" (Genesis 26:7). For a 60-year-old

woman to have this effect, requires more than natural beauty; it requires a supernatural renewal of youth! The Philistine king was also very aware of the desirability of this 60-year-old woman (see Genesis 26:8-11).

Let us go back now to the story of Abraham and Sarah. In Genesis 16, Sarah was 76 and Abraham was 85 (v3). Even up to this age Sarah knew she was fit enough to have children and believed that the reason she had not conceived was that "the Lord has restrained me from bearing children." Therefore she asked Abraham to produce a son through Hagar.

We move forward now to Genesis 17, when Abraham was 99 years old, and Sarah was 90, with both of them too old to have any children. The Lord appeared to Abraham promising him that he will now be a father of many nations. God said, "I will make you exceedingly fruitful; and I will make many nations from you" (see Genesis 17:6). This could only be possible through a supernatural renewal of his youth.

When Abram was ninety-nine years old, the Lord appeared to Abram and said to him, "I am Almighty God; walk before Me and be blameless. And I will make My covenant between Me and you, and will multiply you exceedingly." Then Abram fell on his face, and God talked with him, saying: "As for Me, behold, My covenant is with you, and you shall be a father of many nations. No longer shall your name be called Abram, but your name shall be Abraham; for I have made you a father of many nations. I will make you exceedingly fruitful; and I will make nations of you and kings shall come from you" (Genesis 17:1-6).

Then God said to Abraham, "As for Sarai your wife, you shall not call her name Sarai, but Sarah shall be her name. And I will bless her and also give you a son by her; then I will bless her, and she shall be a mother of nations; kings of peoples shall be from her." Then Abraham fell on his face and laughed, and said in his heart, "Shall a child be born to a man who is one hundred years old? And shall Sarah, who is ninety years old, bear a child?"..."Sarah your wife shall bear you a son, and you shall call his name Isaac..." (Genesis 17:15-19).

This would require an even bigger miracle of youth renewal for Sarah, because at ninety she had to not only conceive but to also sustain a pregnancy to full term and give birth! The promise was confirmed when the Lord visited them again in Genesis 18:10-14, saying:

> *I will certainly return to you according to the time of life, and be-hold, Sarah your wife shall have a son." (Sarah was listening in the tent door which was behind him.) Now Abraham and Sarah were old, well advanced in age; and Sarah had passed the age of childbearing. Therefore Sarah laughed within herself, saying, "After I have grown old, shall I have pleasure, my lord being old also?" And the Lord said to Abraham, "Why did Sarah laugh, saying, 'Shall I surely bear a child, since I am old?' Is anything too hard for the Lord? At the appointed time I will return to you, ac-cording to the time of life, and Sarah shall have a son."*

At this point they meditated upon God's promise and believed God and so received a supernatural renewing of youth and vitality in their bodies, enabling them to reproduce.

Romans 4:17-21 describes Abraham's faith at this time:

> *(as it is written, "I have made you a father of many nations") in the presence of Him whom he believed—God, [1] who gives life to the dead* [he believed in the God who renews our youth!] *and [2] calls those things which do not exist as though they did* (Romans 4:17).

Abraham 1) believed he received God's gift of life into his dying body to renew his youth, and 2) in agreement with God he confessed the promise, calling it into full manifestation.

> *who, contrary to hope, in hope believed* [for the renewing of his youth] *so that he became the father of many nations, according to what was spoken: "So shall your descendents be." And not being weak in faith, he did not consider his own body, already dead (since he was about a hundred years old), and the deadness of Sarah's womb. He did not waver at the promise of God* [for youth renewal] *through unbelief, but was strengthened in faith* [or better: received strength into his body through faith] *giv-ing glory to God* [for bringing it to pass] *and being fully con-vinced that what He had promised He was also able to perform"* (Romans 4:18-21).

This promise for which Abraham is so famous for believing and receiving is the promise of *youth renewal(!),* and his faith is held forth in the Bible as an example for us all! Romans 4:12 says we are to walk in the same steps of faith as Abraham our spiritual father. Then in Romans 4:17-21 we are given this classic example from his life that illustrates the kind of faith that God wants to see operating in us. Therefore the faith we are called to walk in as Abraham's spiritual children includes believing for youth renewal for our physical body!

He 1) believed he received the promise, and 2) confessed it.

So Abraham's youth renewal came through a faith that believed and spoke the Word, which agrees with our key Scripture on youth renewal: He fills our mouths with good things—His words—so that our youth is renewed like the eagle's (see Psalm 103:5). Both their bodies were dead, certainly as far as sexual reproduction was concerned, but they believed in the God who gives life to the dead, for whom nothing is impossible; so through faith they received God's life, strength, and power into their bodies, reenergizing them physically and renewing their youth so that they could give birth to Isaac.

Sarah's faith is described in Hebrews 11:11: "By faith Sarah herself also received [physical] strength (power) to conceive seed, and she bore a child when she was past the age [her youth was renewed], because she judged Him faithful who had promised." She did not just receive power to conceive in her womb, but her whole body had to be renewed in strength and youth for her to sustain a pregnancy and successfully give birth without losing her life (she was 90!). God had to set her clock back many years!

It is clear from the language of Genesis 18 that Sarah conceived very soon after the visit of the Lord. This was also the time of the destruction of Sodom and Gomorrah (see Genesis 19). After that, when Sarah was still early in her pregnancy, Genesis 20:1-2 confirms how much God had renewed Sarah's youth, mentioned previously, in that the king (who could have his pick of young women) sent for Sarah because he wanted to have her for himself. Sarah obviously had to have received a supernatural renewal of her youth! Remember that she was now 90! The power of God had given her a youthful freshness and glow. A few months earlier she had been described as old (see Genesis 18:11). But now it was as if her clock had been rewound 25 years to when Abraham had previously feared for his life because of her beauty, so that again he felt he had to hide the fact he was her husband, thinking that "they will kill me on account of my wife" (Genesis 20:11).

God had to actually step in to stop Abimelech from having relations with her, by revealing that she was already married. Abimelech rightly rebuked Abraham for his deception (see Genesis 20:3-12). To stay alive, Abraham's general policy when traveling was to hide the fact he was married to Sarah because she was so attractive. He had said to Sarah: "This is your kindness that you should do for me: in every place wherever we go, say of me, "He is my brother" (Genesis 20:13). He felt had to maintain this policy—even when she was 90!

Having experienced this renewal of youth, Sarah lived 127 years and Abraham 175 years (see Genesis 23:1; 25:7). Remember, according to Romans 4, both of them had been close to death, when Abraham was 100 and Sarah was 90. So this gave Sarah another 37 years and Abraham 75 years!

We can see that this renewal of youth for Abraham was long lasting, because after Sarah's death (when Abraham was 137), he remarried and had many more children after that! Genesis 25:1-2 says, "Abraham again took a wife, her name was Keturah. And she bore him Zimran, Jokshan, Medan, Midian, Ishbak, and Shuah" (he had other children also, see verse 6). So at 140 years of age, he did not just have the youthfulness to reproduce, but also the desire and strength to start raising another big family. "This is the sum of the years of Abraham's life which he lived: one hundred seventy-five years. Then Abraham breathed his last and died in a good old age, an old man, full of years...." (Genesis 25:7-8).

We are told to walk in the steps of faith of our spiritual father, Abraham (see Romans 4:12), and one of these steps is to believe for youth renewal!

POINTS TO PONDER

1. Connected to God's promises of long life are His promises of youth renewal; for to live long, you surely need your youth to be renewed.

2. The same Holy Spirit who imparted life to the body of Jesus and raised Him from death to life, totally overcoming the

power of death upon Him, now lives and abides in you, and is ready, willing, and able to also give life to your body, mind, and spirit!

3. As you continually draw on God's renewing and healing power and so fulfill your years in health and long life, your life will be a witness and demonstration of His resurrection power.

Chapter 5

THE RENEWAL OF OUR YOUTH, PART II

We have seen that God promises us the renewal of our youth, vitality, and strength (see Psalm 103:5). This is confirmed by Joel 2:25 which says, "I will *restore* to you the *years* that the locust has eaten...." Also Psalm 23:1,3 says, "The Lord is my Shepherd; I shall not want...He *restores* my *soul*." We have seen how God fulfilled this promise for the apostle Paul as well as for Abraham, Sarah, and Rebekah. Now we will see other examples of God fulfilling this promise for those who trust in Him.

YOUTH RENEWAL FOR JOB AND MOSES

God renewed Job's youth when he was 70 years old. Job had a bad year when he lost everything and had a terrible skin disease. He felt he was at death's door and wished he had never been born. But when he repented and humbled himself, God restored and renewed everything he lost, including his youth!

> *...Indeed, the LORD gave Job twice as much as he had before... After this* [bad year] *Job lived one hundred and forty years, and saw his children and grandchildren for four generations. So Job died, old and full of days* (Job 42:10,16-17).

So Job's youth was renewed and he lived another 140 years. So Job must have been 70 when this happened and he received the double of that—another 140 years—so he lived to the ripe old age of 210. You too can believe God for a renewal of your physical strength and mental agility.

God renewed Moses' youth when he was 80 years of age. It must have seemed to Moses that his life was mostly over at 80, after tending sheep in Midian for 40 years. Actually his real work began when he was 80. God empowered him to do a massive job of challenging and beating the superpower of the time and lead Israel on an exodus out of Egypt. Under God he also governed the nation of two million people and wrote their laws and organized their worship. God truly renewed his youthful strength! After spending time with God on the holy mountain, his face was shining with the glory of God (see Exodus 34:29-35). Spending time in God's presence will also renew *your* youth!

We see the result of God renewing Moses' youth in Deuteronomy 34:7: "Moses was one hundred twenty years old when he died. His eyes were not dim nor was his natural vigor diminished." Moses lived until 120, but he clearly could have lived much longer, as there was nothing physically wrong with him. The only reason he died then was because of God's discipline in not letting him enter the Promised Land because of his sin in striking the rock in anger when God told him just to speak to it. There is an aging process at work, but we can trust God to keep us from sickness and renew our youth and strength like Moses, so we can live a full, long, and fruitful life on earth.

YOUTH RENEWAL FOR CALEB AND JOSHUA

It is clear that God also renewed Caleb's youth. He said in Joshua 14:7,10-12:

> *I was forty years old when Moses the servant of the LORD sent me from Kadesh Barnea to spy out the land, and I brought back word to him as it was in my heart. And now, behold, the LORD has kept me alive, as He said, these forty-five years, ever since the Lord spoke this word to Moses while Israel wandered in the wilderness; and now, here I am this day, eight-five years old. As yet I am as strong this day as on the day that Moses sent me; just as my strength was then, so now is my strength for war, both for going out and for coming in. Now therefore, give me this mountain of which the LORD spoke in that day; for you heard in that*

day how the Anakim were there, and that the cities were great and fortified. It may be that the LORD will be with me, and I shall be able to drive them out as the LORD said.

Joshua lived to the good age of 110 (see Joshua 24:29, Judges 2:8). The best estimate that fits all the information in the Bible is that Joshua died about 13 years after the division of the land, and so he was about 97 at the time of Joshua 13:1: "Now [at the time of the division] Joshua was old, advanced in years. And the LORD said to him: 'You are old, advanced in years.'" He must have been significantly older than Caleb, who at this same time (at age 85) was not described as old like Joshua, but was still very active and going strong (see Joshua 14:10-12). This means that Joshua was about 90 when he led the dynamic invasion of the Promised Land, for it took about seven years until the land was divided. Therefore he was about 50 years old when he led the fighting against the Amelekites in the year of the Exodus, 40 years earlier (see Exodus 17). Surely God renewed Joshua's youth and strength!

One key to this renewal is seen in Exodus 33:11: "The LORD spoke to Moses face to face, as a man speaks to his friend. And he would return to the camp, but his servant *Joshua* the son of Nun, a *young man*, did not depart from the tabernacle." Joshua loved to spend time in the presence and glory of the Lord, which caused the renewal of his life. Notice that at the time of Exodus 33:11 (the year of the exodus) Joshua, at the age of about 50 years, is described as a young man!

YOUTH RENEWAL FOR KING HEZEKIAH

One of the greatest examples of someone receiving the renewal of his youth, and as a result the lengthening of his life, is King Hezekiah. He received a dramatic renewal of his life. This involved one of the greatest miracles in the Bible.

Isaiah 38:1 says, "In those days Hezekiah was sick and near death [he was only about 40]. And Isaiah the prophet, the son of Amoz, went to him and said to him, 'Thus says the Lord: 'Set your house in order, for you shall die and not live.'" It was not God's will that he should die young, as we shall see in the miracle God does to restore him. Actually, God sent Isaiah to point out the reality of King Hezekiah's situation, so that he would get serious and seek God with all his heart. God wanted to get him out of his spiritual passivity, so that he would fight for his life, for it was the wrong time for him to die. God was saying, "As things are now, you are going to die!"

This got the king's attention! Isaiah 38:2 says, "Then Hezekiah turned his face toward the wall, and prayed to the Lord." This showed his determination to turn his back on everything else and seek God until he got an answer from heaven. The next verse says that he prayed, "'Remember now, O LORD, I pray, how I have walked before You in truth and with a loyal heart, and have done what is good in Your sight.' And Hezekiah wept bitterly." His weeping signified his deep confession and repentance for sin. Later when Hezekiah looked back at how he had miraculously recovered from his sickness, he talked about how God forgave him all his sins as a result of this humble confession:

> ...So You will restore me and make me live. Indeed it was for my own peace that I had great bitterness; but You have lovingly delivered my soul from the pit of corruption, for You have cast all my sins behind Your back [out of sight] (Isaiah 38:16-17).

Through confession and believing prayer, Hezekiah put himself into position to receive the wonderful miracle of a renewal of his youth, so that he would live and not die.

> And the word of the LORD came to Isaiah, saying, "Go and tell Hezekiah, 'Thus says the LORD, the God of David your father: "I have heard your prayer, I have seen your tears; surely I will add to your days fifteen years. I will also deliver you and this city from the hand of the king of Assyria, and I will defend this city'" (Isaiah 38:4-6).

As well as his life-threatening sickness, the king was also under the imminent threat of destruction by the invading Assyrians; but through prevailing prayer, God saved and lengthened his life. Hezekiah repented with tears and God forgave him, restored his health, delivered him from death, and renewed his life, giving him another 15 years of life and kingship.

The situation was especially serious because he was childless at the time. His eldest son, Manasseh, was 12 when he became king after Hezekiah's death (see 2 Kings 21:1). This means Manasseh was born three years after God restored Hezekiah's life from certain death. Had

Hezekiah died without a son, that would have ended the kingly line from David and Solomon, out of which the Messiah, the son of David, was to come. So this was a very serious situation: not only were they under threat from Assyria, but Hezekiah's sickness threatened the Messianic seed-line. His premature death would have endangered the house of David and also the coming of the Messiah-King! These are further reasons why Hezekiah prayed so earnestly for God to heal him and rewind the clock (renew his youth).

God needs our faith and prayers to fulfill His plan for our lives. It is interesting that even with all this at stake, God still needed Hezekiah to turn to Him and call upon Him for life, which is why He sent Isaiah to provoke him out of passivity. Just like Hezekiah, if we are facing death and God's plan for us has not yet been fulfilled, we need to rise out of our passivity and get serious with God, turning away from all other things and seeking God alone, repenting and calling out to Him with all our hearts for Him to heal and renew our lives, just as Hezekiah turned his face to the wall, praying to God.

In view of the momentous nature of these events, it is no surprise that God also performed an outstanding sign in the heavens, in conjunction with the miraculous renewing of Hezekiah's life. This sign wonderfully illustrated what God had done for Hezekiah. Isaiah 38:7-9 says:

> *And this is the sign to you from the Lord, that the Lord will do this thing which He has spoken: "Behold, I will bring the shadow on the sundial, which has gone down with the sun on the sundial of Ahaz, ten degrees [steps] backward." So the sun returned 10 degrees [steps] on the dial by which it had gone down. This is the writing of Hezekiah king of Judah, when he had been sick and had recovered from his sickness.*

Each degree or step on the sundial measured one hour. So this means that God moved the sun backward in its course by ten hours! So Hezekiah was healed near the end of the day, let us say at about 6 P.M., with the sun about to set. This represented Hezekiah's life that was about to end. The sun was about to set on his life, his day on earth was about to end. Then God did a miracle! He turned the clock back ten hours; He moved the sun to its position ten hours earlier, to where it was at 8 a.m. when the day was just starting. In effect God doubled the length of the daylight; He renewed the day giving it a fresh start. This was exactly what He did for Hezekiah's life, He turned his clock back 15 years, renewing his youth and giving him a brand-new start. Before he prayed, his life was about to end, but God heard his prayer and gave him another 15 years to fulfill His will. As a result, the length of his reign was doubled from about 14 to 29 years.

The Assyrians were then miraculously defeated by the angel of the Lord (see Isaiah 36,37). Hezekiah was able to give birth to his first-born, Manasseh, from whom Christ was descended.

HE CAN REWIND YOUR CLOCK

This was one of the great miracles of the Bible. Just as God stopped the sun for Joshua, God moved the sun back ten hours for Hezekiah to show that He was putting his clock back and giving him a new start, and that's what He wants to do for you. You may feel like Hezekiah, that most of your life is over, that the sun is about to set on your life before you have lived out the full number of your days. But if you will seek God like Hezekiah, He will hear you and rewind your clock, releasing new life to you, renewing your youth, and giving you a fresh start so that a new day will dawn for your life. He will lengthen your life if you ask Him.

The promise of youth renewal is not just for these men and women of the Bible, it is one of the covenant benefits that belong to all of God's people (see Psalm 103:5). It is available to all, but we have to call out to God in faith and receive it. These biblical examples are given to encourage and inspire us to believe for God's life and power to work in our physical bodies. God is no respecter of persons. He said, "I will pour out My Spirit on *all flesh*" (see Joel 2:28, Acts 2:17). He does not just want to impart life into our spirits, but to all of our flesh (including our body and mind)!

We must *believe and speak* God's power into our bodies! Believe (receive) God's power into your body and speak (call) it into manifestation. Other examples of God releasing His supernatural power and strength into people's physical bodies are Samson (see Judges 14-16), enabling him to do many mighty feats; David's mighty men, operating in supernatural ability and strength (see 2 Samuel 23:8-39, 1 Chronicles 11:10-47); and Elijah (see 1 Kings 18:45-46), enabling him to overtake Ahab's chariot and horses after interceding for an outpouring of rain.

The key to the blessing of youth renewal (staying evergreen) is trusting in God rather than in ourselves:

> *Cursed is the man who trusts in man, and makes flesh his strength, whose heart departs from the Lord. For he shall be like a shrub in the desert [he will dry up], and shall not see when good comes, but shall inhabit the parched places in the wilderness, in a salt land which is not inhabited* (Jeremiah 17:5-6).

But on the other hand:

> *Blessed is the man who trusts in the Lord, whose hope is the Lord. For he shall be like a tree planted by the waters, which spreads out its roots by the river, and will not fear when heat comes; but its leaf will [always] be green, and will not be anxious in the year of drought, nor will cease from yielding fruit* (Jeremiah 17:7-8).

Through trusting in God, we are able to constantly draw life (water) from the Lord, renewing our health, life, and youth, so that we stay evergreen and fruitful in all circumstances.

Psalm 1:1-3 gives the same picture, emphasizing that the key to being able to trust God and receive His renewing life is continual meditation on His Word:

> *Blessed is the man...[whose] delight is in the law of the Lord, and in His law he meditates day and night. He shall be like a tree planted by the rivers of water, that brings forth its fruit in its season, whose leaf shall not wither [this is renewed youth]; and whatever he does shall prosper.*

THE BENEFITS OF THE LORD

Psalm 103 tells us about the benefits of the Lord to us: "Bless the Lord, O my soul; and all that is within me, bless His holy name! Bless the Lord, O my soul, and forget not *all His benefits*" (Psalm 103:1-2). God's gracious benefits available to all believers include:

1. Full forgiveness
2. Total healing

3. Redemption from the curse (deliverance from destruction and an early death)

4. Crowning us with His life and covenant blessings

5. The renewal of our youth

It is the Lord:

1. Who *forgives* all your iniquities

2. Who *heals* all your diseases

3. Who *redeems* your life from destruction (the curse)

4. Who *crowns* you with lovingkindness and tender mercies

5. Who *satisfies* your mouth with good things, so that your *youth is renewed* like the eagle's (see Psalm 103:3-5).

All of these benefits result in the lengthening of our lives.

How can we receive and activate these benefits in our lives? We must:

1. *Discover* what all His benefits are from His Word

2. *Remember* them (bring them to the forefront of our minds)

3. *Thank* (bless) God for them (see Psalm 103:1-2).

We are to bless God with our praise and thanksgiving; but as we do this, we must not forget to bless Him for all of His benefits (blessings) to us. In other words, we must remember them and acknowledge (name) them all, thanking God for them with our hearts and lips. That is exactly what the psalmist goes on to do in verses 3-5 in Psalm 103.

Psalm 103 tells us to bless God for *all* His benefits and that these benefits include healing and the renewal of our youth. Therefore we are to thank God for His promises of healing, renewal, and long life. In fact, it is as we thank God in faith for these blessings and confess them over our lives that they start to become activated and manifested in our lives. In particular, the promise of the renewal of our youth is closely connected and related to the words of our mouths: "Who satisfies [fills] your mouth with good things, so that your youth [vitality] is renewed like the eagle's" (Psalm 103:5).

God gives (feeds) us with good things—His promises—so that as our mouths are filled with His words, their goodness and life is released to us renewing our strength and youth. So a major key for our youth to be renewed is to fill our mouths with God's good promises for our life, confessing His Word over our lives, and giving thanks for every promised blessing. If we fill our mouths with His words (His promises of life), then our youth will be renewed like the eagle's. Thus we are to eat (believe and receive) these promises for ourselves and speak them out, and they will start to come to pass in us.

IN WEAKNESS WE ARE STRONG

Joel 3:10 says, "Let the [physically] weak *say, 'I am strong'*" [in the strength of the Lord]. This seems like a paradox. Why should the weak say they are strong? Because it is through confessing God's promises of life, that His strength is released in us and our youth is renewed. When we are weak in ourselves, we are to come to God in faith and receive His strength, and then *say* we are *strong* in His power. As we believe and speak His promises of life, His strength is manifested in us. We are not to wait until we feel strong before we confess it, for it is the weak who are to say they are strong. It is in our very weakness we are to say, *"I am strong, for the Lord's strength, power, and life is working in me."* Again we see that a major key to the supernatural renewing and restoring of our youth and strength is to speak the Word.

Previously we discussed how Paul often faced weakness and death in his tests and trials, but as he learned to trust God in these situations, he found that the life of Jesus was then manifested in his body (see 2 Corinthians 4:7-12). In Second Corinthians 4:13-14 he adds insight into how this life and power is released through faith:

> *Since we have the same spirit of faith* [as the Messiah], *according to what is written, "I believed and therefore I spoke"* [from Psalm 116:10], *we also believe and therefore speak, knowing that He who raised up the Lord Jesus will also raise us up with Jesus, and will present us with you."*

Psalm 116:9-10 describes the faith of the Messiah (Christ) in facing death. He declares: "I will walk before the LORD in the land of the living. I believed, therefore I spoke." He believed in God's resurrection

59

power for Him, and in that spirit of faith He also spoke it (the promise of life). He released His faith by His words, and God raised Him to life.

In Second Corinthians 4:13-14, Paul is saying that we are to move in the same spirit of faith as Jesus, believing and speaking life in the face of weakness, sickness, and death, knowing that the same God who raised up Jesus will also raise us up by His power. It is by believing and speaking God's Word that God's resurrection life is released to renew our youth!

Romans 10:9-10 says, "If you confess with your mouth Jesus as Lord and believe in your heart that God has raised Him from the dead, you will be saved [blessed]. For with the heart one believes unto righteousness, and with the mouth *confession* is made unto salvation" [manifestation].

I encourage you to declare boldly:

- I shall not die young, but live long, and declare the works of the LORD (see Psalm 118:17).

- The LORD is *my strength* and song, and He has become my salvation (see Exodus 15:2).

- The LORD is my light and my salvation; whom shall I fear? The LORD is *the strength of my life*; of whom shall I be afraid? (see Psalm 27:1).

- *I am strong* in the strength of the Lord (see Joel 3:10).

- Thanks be to God, who gives me the victory over death through my Lord Jesus Christ (see 1 Corinthians 15:57).

- God has not given me a spirit of fear, but of power and of love and of a sound mind (see 2 Timothy 1:7).

- The same Spirit of Him who raised Jesus from the dead dwells in me, and so He shall also quicken (give life to) my mortal body by His Spirit in me (see Romans 8:11).

- Christ has redeemed me from the curse (of sickness and an early death), having become a curse for me (for it is written, "Cursed is everyone who hangs on a tree"), that the blessing of Abraham (which includes health and long life) might come upon me in Christ (see Galatians 3:13-14).

- The LORD is my Shepherd; I shall not want (He provides all my needs, including the renewal of my strength and youth). He makes me to lie down in green pastures; He leads me beside the still waters. He restores my soul; He leads me in the paths of righteousness for His name's sake. Yea, though I walk through the valley of the shadow of death, I will fear no evil; for You are with me (to bring me through the danger, and to keep me safe); Your rod and Your staff, they comfort me. You prepare a table (of blessings, including healing, the children's bread) before me in the presence of my enemies; You anoint my head with oil (the anointing of the Spirit); My cup runs over (with abundant life). Surely goodness and mercy (His covenant blessings, including renewal of youth and long life) shall follow me all the days of my life; and I will dwell in the house of the LORD forever (see Psalm 23).

- God will satisfy me with long life and show me His salvation (see Psalm 91:16).

- Through Jesus I have an abundant, long life (see John 10:10).

- My mouth is filled with the goodness of God's Word, so my youth is being renewed as the eagle (see Psalm 103:5).

- The Resurrection Life of Christ is working in me. *I will live and not die.* I will live to a full age. With long life I will be satisfied. I will see God's salvation.

Another way we can fill our mouths with good things, and so have our youth renewed, is by speaking in tongues: "For with stammering lips and another tongue He will speak to this people, to whom He said, 'This is the rest with which you may cause the weary to rest,' and, 'This is the refreshing'" (Isaiah 28:11-12, which is quoted in First Corinthians 14:21 and applied there to speaking in tongues, which is a supernatural prayer language available to all believers through the Holy Spirit; see Acts 2:4).

When we speak in tongues we allow the Spirit to refresh and rest us, renewing our lives spiritually, mentally, and physically. Isaiah 12:1-6 confirms that believers can draw (bring forth) the waters of salvation into their lives, from the Holy Spirit within their spirits, and they do this by their words:

> *In that Day* [of the New Covenant] *you will say* [confess]: *"O Lord, I will praise You. Though You were angry with me, Your anger is turned away* [by the Atonement], *and You comfort me. Behold, God is my salvation, I will trust and not be afraid; for the Lord is my strength and song; He also has become my salvation." Therefore, with joy [rejoicing] you will draw water* [life] *from the wells* [springs] *of salvation* [within us] (Isaiah 12:1-3).

Since we have received Him within as our salvation, we can now release the waters of salvation into our lives by joyfully speaking His words of life in praise, thanksgiving, singing, confession, witnessing, and prayer. This is how we draw the waters of life from the springs of salvation (our reborn spirit):

> *And in that day you will say:* **"Praise the LORD,** *call upon His Name; declare His deeds among the peoples,* **make mention** *that His name is exalted.* **Sing to the Lord,** *for He has done excellent things; this is known in all the earth.* **Cry out and shout,** *O inhabitant of Zion* [all believers are citizens of Heaven], *for great is the* **Holy One** *of Israel in your midst!"* (Isaiah 12:4-6).

This last phrase gives the key to the whole dynamic process—the Greater One, the Holy Spirit of God Himself now lives within us! He lives in our spirits, filling our well with His living waters, so as we joyfully speak His Word in faith, we release His living waters to flow out of our spirits. Thus we draw (bring forth) waters of life and healing from the wells of salvation.

POINTS TO PONDER

1. There is an aging process at work, but you can trust God to keep you from sickness and renew your youth and strength, like Moses, so you can live a full, long, and fruitful life on earth.

2. Bless God with your praise and thanksgiving; do not forget to bless Him for all of His benefits (blessings). You

must remember them and acknowledge (name) them all, thanking God for them with your heart and lips.

3. Believe and speak God's Word so that God's resurrection life is released to renew your youth!

Chapter 6

THE BIBLE DEFINITION
OF LONG LIFE

What is long life according to the Bible? What can we believe for? What is the proper (full) number of (our) days allotted to us? How long is full age?

Many Christians believe the Bible tells us that long life is 70 or 80 years and so are not expecting to live any longer, and so when they reach 60, many are already winding down. The Scripture they base this belief on is Psalm 90:10: "The days of our lives are seventy years; and if by reason of strength they are eighty years." However on closer study we will see that this is by no means the general maximum life span for believers.

Psalm 90 was written by Moses; its heading is: "A Prayer of Moses the man of God" (v1). It describes the condition of Israel wandering in the wilderness for 40 years when in unbelief they refused to enter the Promised Land. They were under a special curse according to Numbers 14:29-30, which said that all those over 20 who had sinned would die in the wilderness (within 40 years) and not enter the Land. Thus their life span was cut short by this judgment.

The curse is described in Psalm 90 as God's wrath and judgment bringing early death on that unbelieving generation:

You carry them away [to death] *like a flood. They are like a sleep. In the morning they are like grass which grows up: In the morning it flourishes and grows up; in the evening it is cut down and withers. For we have been consumed by Your anger, and by*

Your wrath we are terrified. You have set our iniquities before You, our secret sins in the light of Your countenance. For all our days have passed away in Your wrath; we finish our years like a sigh. The days of our lives are 70 years; and if by reason of strength they are 80 years, yet their boast is only labor and sorrow; for it is soon cut off, and we fly away. Who knows the power of Your anger? For as the fear of You, so is Your wrath. So teach us to number our days, that we may gain a heart of wisdom (Psalm 90:5-12).

So this well-known passage in Psalm 90 that seems to define a full life span as 70-80 years actually describes a specific generation of Israel that were under a curse due to their sin. Although Psalm 90:10 says: "The days of our lives are 70 years; and if by reason of strength they are 80 years," Psalm 90 describes life for the generation of Israel who refused to enter the Promised Land through unbelief. As a result they were doomed to wander the rest of their lives in the wilderness and to die before Israel entered the Land 40 years later. As a result, this limited their life spans to about 70-80 years. So 70 or 80 years is not the general maximum life span for believers. And it certainly does not apply to New Testament believers under the blessing of God!

Joshua, Caleb, and Moses, who all believed, did not live under this curse, and so they all lived to well past 100. We saw that Moses himself lived until 120 and even then he was in full strength and could have lived longer. So surely Moses did not mean to say 70-80 was a general maximum life span. In fact, Moses is lamenting as he sees the people all dying unnaturally young around him because of the curse. It is clear that people were used to living much longer, and Moses is distressed at seeing people die at only 70 and 80, which he considers to be sadly young! So Moses ends the psalm with a prayer for the ending of the curse, that the people of God will be able to enjoy full and fruitful lives again in the Promised Land:

Return, O LORD! How long? And have compassion on Your servants. Oh, satisfy us early with Your mercy, that we may rejoice and be glad all our days! Make us glad according to the days in which You have afflicted us, the years in which we have seen evil. Let Your work appear to Your servants, and Your glory to their children. And let the beauty of the LORD our God be upon us, and establish the work of our hands for us; yes, estab-lish the work of our hands (Psalm 90:13-17).

So Psalm 90 describes life and life spans under the curse. Moses went on to write Psalm 91, which describes God's will and plan for His people under His blessing—a long and satisfying life! For in Psalm 91:16, God Himself says, "with long life will I satisfy him." God wants you to live a full and long and healthy life until you are satisfied, then your spirit can leave your body and go to God.

These two psalms of Moses (90 and 91) form a contrasting pair. Psalm 90 shows believers under discipline for stubborn unbelief and disobedience having their lives cut short so that they died before reaching 70-80 years old. In contrast, Psalm 91 shows believers under the blessing of God being satisfied with long life. It is Psalm 91, not Psalm 90, that is the norm for believers today who are living in fellowship with God, living under the shadow (protection) of His wings.

REDEEMED FROM THE CURSE

Thus the limit of 70 years was for an unbelieving, cursed people and certainly does not apply to a believing New Testament Christian who is under the blessing of God. As for us, we have been *redeemed from the curse* by Christ, who took the curse of early death for us, by dying on the Cross, so that we can now live under the blessing of Abraham, who enjoyed a long and full life of 175 years, through receiving the promise by faith (see Galatians 3:13-14).

Part of the curse that Jesus bore for us was an early death. He was only 33.5 years of age when He died. He suffered the curse of an early death, so we could have the promised blessing of a long and blessed life. He took the curse of a life cut short, so that we could live in the blessing of long life. He did it for us, paying the price in full, so we should honor Him by receiving all that He has done.

Psalm 91:1 describes this blessing that is available to us: "He who dwells in the secret place of the Most High shall abide under the shadow of the Almighty." In Psalm 91:14-16, God Himself speaks these wonderful promises to us:

Because he has set his love on Me, I will deliver him: I will set him on high, for he has known My name. He will call on me, and I will answer him: I will be with him in trouble; I will deliver him, and honor him. With long life will I satisfy him, and show him My salvation.

To satisfy means to be full. God wants us to be satisfied with long life and for it not to be cut short. So if we are not satisfied with 70 years, then we can go on to 80, 90, 100, and even more until we are satisfied! Of course we cannot live forever in this mortal body, but we can live a life full of days, rather than it being cut short. Now this is not just a promise about living a long time, it is about us maintaining our basic health and sound mentality into old age, because if we lose that, we would surely not be satisfied with our lives, would we?! So when God says, with long life I will satisfy him, He is not just saying He will give us a long life, but that we will be satisfied with our lives because we will be in the blessing of God and basically be in a sound condition.

Many people now live past 80 and increasingly people live to be over 100. In fact, 80 is now only the average age. So 70-80 cannot be God's measure of a full or maximum age. If we make the mistake of believing 70 to be our limit, we will expect and plan to decline as we approach that age and to die soon after. If we think 70 is old age, then even as a relative youngster in our 40s we will start thinking of ourselves as middle-aged and on our way down. As a person thinks in his heart so he is (see Proverbs 23:7). As a result of this thinking we will become passive, inviting death. Actually the Bible sets a much different limit. We must actively believe for and plan to fulfill our number of years (to live out our full life span).

So what is the true biblical measure of humankind's life span? Originally man was not designed to die at all; his cells and organs would regenerate perfectly. But sin brought death: God warned Adam that from the day he sinned against God he would start to experience death, saying "you will surely die," literally: "dying you shall die" (see Genesis 2:17). Disconnected from God, he immediately died spiritually, and death also started to work in his body also, through sin, although he lived for another 930 years. Death disrupted his life source and regeneration, limiting how many times cells could be copied.

Before the Flood, man's life span was almost 1,000 years. Methuselah lived the longest—969 years! However at Noah's flood, God shortened man's life span to a maximum of 120 years to restrain the spread of sin. Genesis 6:3 says, "The LORD said, 'My Spirit shall not strive with man forever, for he is indeed flesh: yet his days shall be one hundred and twenty years.'" In Genesis 6 God is describing His judgment that He was about to bring upon humankind due to the terrible worldwide spread of sin, evil, and violence, and in that connection He also reduced man's maximum full life span to 120 years. Here God is announcing He will not always strive with man, but is giving him at most 120 years of grace to repent and turn to God—for after death it is too late for people to get right with God. This change began to take effect at the Flood, and it has not been changed since, so it still applies today.

Now one interpretation of these 120 years is that this warning was given to humankind 120 years before the Flood, and so it applies only to the people who lived before the Flood. Thus God was warning them that the Flood would fall in 120 years.

I am quite happy to accept that Genesis 6:3 was a 120-year warning of the Flood. However it is not limited to this, for it clearly reads as a general statement that applies to all of humankind: My Spirit shall not always strive with man, for he also is flesh: yet his days shall be 120 years. This is a general limitation on human life spans that applies to all humankind, both before and after the Flood. It is one of many changes brought in at this time.

This interpretation is confirmed by the biblical evidence that life spans began to get shorter after the Flood, settling down to a maximum of 120 years. Moreover it is confirmed by present biological fact that 120 is the effective maximum for a human life span. People have been known to live this long, but not much longer. Thus seeing 70 or 80 as the maximum expected length of a life is not true to biblical or scientific fact (it is actually just the average life span now). Therefore if we are walking in the blessing of God, we should not limit our expectancy to 70 or 80 good years of health and life. God has measured a full human life span as 120 years, which may seem a lot, but actually it was a major cut back. Science confirms that the cells in our body are programmed to continue to replicate for about 120 years but no more, so that even in the absence of sickness this is an effective maximum age.

So at the Flood, God shortened life spans to a maximum of 120 years. He either did this directly, by reprogramming man's genetics for a shorter life cycle, or indirectly through the changes to the conditions on earth brought about by the Flood (or both). Before the Flood conditions of climate and nutrition were perfect. But after the Flood conditions on earth were much more hostile with a greater exposure to ultraviolet radiation and such a drastic decrease of good nutrition from plants that it was necessary for God to sanction the killing of animals for food. A shorter, sped-up life span was a way for humankind to adapt for survival in these worse conditions, because it also meant we could reproduce much faster. Thus the yardstick by which we should measure the length of a human life span is 120 years. That is our true potential, not 70 years. If 120 rather than 70 is the full measure of a person's life, then that will change the way you think about your life. It does not mean you have to live to 120, but that is the effective limit, rather than 70 or 80. Actually 70 is mid-life—just past halfway.

If you think you have 70 years maximum, then when you reach 50-60 you will already start to think of yourself as getting old, expecting to decline and wind down and then die soon, and your body will pick up those signals from your mind. Your mind and body are very closely connected. What happens in your body is directly connected to what is happening in your mind. Bad thoughts and attitudes in the mind cause harmful chemicals to be released into the body and brain causing depression and sickness; while good, joyful thoughts release healthy chemicals. "A merry heart does good, like medicine, but a broken spirit dries the bones" (Proverbs 17:22). "A sound heart is life to the body, but envy is rottenness to the bones" (Proverbs 14:30).

So if your mind is telling your body that you are getting old, you don't have long to live, your body picks up those signals and conforms itself to them. If you think of yourself as old and in decline, you will become passive, and your body and mind will adjust to your beliefs by slowing down and aging ahead of time (see Proverbs 23:7).

But if you measure your life against 120, then at 50-60 you will think of yourself as just approaching mid-life and you will be expecting many more good vigorous years serving God, and your mind will program your body accordingly. So we need to renew our minds with the Word that a full life span is 120 years, and so we have many good years ahead. If 100-120 is the real definition of old age, then 60 is only mid-life, not old age!

When Reheboam started to reign at age 41, he was considered to be a young man (compare 1 Kings 14:21 and 12:8). We saw in Exodus 33:11 that Joshua, at 50, was called a young man! At this time he was on the frontline whenever Israel fought a battle! He was 90 when he led the invasion of the Promised Land. Look at Moses who only really got started at 80! So in comparison, you are still a youngster!

Let God renew your youth like an eagle so that you can rise up with new wings to new heights in God! He is no respecter of persons and so wants to give you the same youthful vigor and good mentality as these men of God had in their later years. So do not re-tire from God's work, rather *re-fire*, unless by re-tire you are thinking of yourself as a car!

When you look at an aircraft, you think it could never leave the ground, because the law of gravity would keep it down. Likewise you might think your life could never lift off again. But as a plane moves forward, the law of lift overcomes the law of gravity. Likewise we can move forward, trusting in Christ's life to renew and lift us: "The law of the Spirit of life in Christ Jesus has made me free from the law of sin and death" [that pulls us down] (Romans 8:2). With our wings of faith stretched out to receive the action of the wind of the Spirit, we will start to rise up on wings as an eagle (see Isaiah 40:31). We resist death by constantly laying hold of His resurrection life that overcame death. We can believe God for a renewal of our physical and mental strength (youth).

Declare with the psalmist: "I shall not die [young], but live [long], and declare the works of the Lord" (Psalm 118:17).

POINTS TO PONDER

1. The limit of 70-80 years in Psalm 90 was imposed on life spans as a result of a special curse upon the wilderness generation, so does not apply to believers today. We have been redeemed from the curse and are under the blessing of God, which includes long life.

2. Moses wrote Psalm 90 to describe those under the curse, but in contrast he wrote Psalm 91 to describe believers

under the blessing (under the shadow of the Most High), which concludes with: *"With long life will I satisfy him"* (Psalm 91:16). This long life must be longer than 70 years. Moses himself lived to 120 years old, and was strong and healthy to the end.

3. Jesus has redeemed us from the curse of an early death, by taking that curse for us, by suffering an early death, that we might enjoy the promised blessing of a long and blessed life.

4. It is confirmed by present biological fact that 120 is the effective maximum for a human life span.

5. Let God renew your youth like an eagle so that you can rise up with new wings to new heights in God! He wants to give you youthful vigor and good mentality.

Chapter 7

FIGHT FOR YOUR LIFE!

We have seen that God's will is for us to have a long and full life. In Psalm 91:16, God's promise for those who dwell in the secret place of the Almighty is: "With *long life* I will *satisfy* him, and show him My salvation." We saw long life can be as much as 120 years. However the length of our life depends on our believing and our living. Although God gives a promise of long life to believers, it is not automatic. We have to lay hold of it by faith and claim it, rather than have a passive attitude that says, *"When it's my time to go, I will go. There is nothing I can do about it."* This attitude is an unbiblical fatalism, as discussed in Chapter 3.

There is a war over our lives, and we have to fight the fight of faith. Jesus said in John 10:10 that we have an enemy: "The thief does not come except to steal, and to kill, and to destroy. I [Jesus] have come that they may have life, and that they may have it more abundantly." Here Jesus reveals satan's threefold strategy for our lives. The thief wants to:

1. *steal* blessings from our lives

2. *kill*, that is to cause us to die young

3. *destroy* us eternally, that is to take us to everlasting hell with him.

So if you are a true believer in Christ you have already won the main victory over him. You have passed from death to life! Eternal life is yours, praise God! Nevertheless, satan is still out to steal and to kill, to spoil both the quality and quantity (length) of our lives. His main weapon is deception. He wants to fool you into believing that you will die young, that you can only expect to live 60 or 70 years, that you are getting old at 40 or 50.

Satan wants you to passively accept it is out of your hands, and accept an early death. The Bible says, as people think in their hearts, so they are (see Proverbs 23:7). If you believe and speak satan's lies, you give him power over you, but if you believe and speak God's Word, satan's power is nullified. If a thief came to your house, you would resist him. Likewise by faith we have to resist satan and the spirit of death. It is well known that fighters with a strong will to live, live longer.

Although satan, through his lies, is trying to cut our lives short, Jesus is much more powerful, and He has come to give us His abundant life, to overcome satan's plan in all three areas. His life in us is more than enough to overcome every attack of satan.

So although satan comes to steal our blessings in this life, Jesus came to give us a good life of abundant blessings. Although satan wants to kill and cut our life short, Jesus offers to give us an abundantly long life on this earth. Although satan wants to see us destroyed in hell, Jesus gives us eternal life with Him. So John 10:10 is a promise that Jesus offers us: 1) a good, strong life; 2) a long life; and 3) eternal life. He came to give us: 1) the abundant life of blessings now; 2) an abundance of long life; and 3) eternal life.

Abundance means more than enough, like a river that overflows its banks. So Jesus has come that satan's plans for your life will fail and you will have an abundantly long life. Jesus said that although satan comes to steal, kill, and destroy, He (Jesus) came to give us abundant life: a full, long life on earth as well as eternal life. His abundant life does not just overcome death in our spirit and soul, but it is also for our bodies.

THE FIGHT OF FAITH

So we are in the middle of a *battle* for our lives. On the one side stands the thief who wants to steal, kill, and destroy. On the other side stands the Lord Jesus who want us to have an abundance of life. We stand in the middle and we choose between life or death. It is our choice—do we believe in satan's lies and follow his ways (and receive his death), or do we believe in Jesus and follow His ways (and receive

His life)? We must not be passive, but actively choose to believe in Jesus and His promises of life, and walk in His Word.

If we are passive, we will fall prey to the lies of the enemy. We have to actively submit to God and to His Word, and resist satan and his lies: "Therefore submit to God. *Resist* the devil and he will flee from you" (James 4:7). We have to put forth effort in this spiritual battle. There is a fight we must fight or else we will lose: "we do not wrestle against flesh and blood, but against principalities, against powers" (Ephesians 6:12).

We have to "fight the good fight of faith" (1 Timothy 6:12). Don't be a wimp; fight the good fight! First Timothy 6:12 literally says, "Fight the good fight of *the* faith." There is a necessary fight in the Christian life. What is this fight of faith that we are commanded to fight?

A fight implies we must put forth great effort. What kind of effort must we make in order to succeed in this fight? The fight of faith is the fight to believe and stand on the Word and possess the promises. We must put forth effort against enemy resistance to believe, hold on to, and keep hold of God's Word. That's why it is literally the fight of *the faith*. The faith is the full revelation of God that we are called to believe. Thus *the faith* is *the Word* of God, which He has given to us and is written in the Bible.

So the fight of the faith is the fight of the Word of God. It is the fight to know, believe, receive, and hold on to the Word, whatever comes against us from the world, the flesh, or the devil in the form of doubts, setbacks, lies, afflictions, or circumstances. It is not just a fight over the Word (promise), but we shall see that it is also a fight that we must fight with the Word. The fight of faith is a fight that is about our faith (whether we *believe* and maintain our *faith* in the Word) and it is also a fight we fight using our faith.

Notice that it is a *good* fight. The Greek word here conveys the meaning of a fight fought with excellence of technique resulting in a successful outcome. It is a good fight with good results. It is a good fight because it is a fight we will always win, if we do it God's way. It is not fighting other Christians in strife and gossip! That would be a bad fight! Faith works through love (see Galatians 5:6), so if we fight the wrong fight (fighting people) and do not walk in love, our faith will fail, and we open the door to satan and lose the fight of faith. We don't fight people; we stand on God's Word and resist satan when he tries to move us away from it.

That is why we need to be strong in God's power. Again, Ephesians 6:10-12 says, "Be strong in the Lord, and in the power of His might. Put on the whole armor of God, that you may stand against the wiles of the devil. For we do not wrestle against flesh and blood, but [we wrestle] against principalities, against powers." The fight of the faith is really a fight over the place of the Word in our lives. Fighting the good fight of "the faith" is to maintain a firm hold (faith-grip) on God's promises to us. Jesus offers us His *life*, a life that has already overcome and defeated death in all its forms, and He promises it to us in His Word, but we have to forcefully lay hold of His life by faith: "Fight the good fight of the faith, lay hold on eternal life" [the life of God] (1 Timothy 6:12). How do we lay hold of His life? By laying hold of His Word (His promise of life)! His life is in His Word, so if we want to lay hold of His life, we have to lay hold of His Word and never let it go.

Imagine you are holding on to something very precious that belongs to you, and someone comes and tries to persuade you to let it go and give it to him. If you refuse, he then tries to pull it out of your hand. What will you do? Will you be a wimp and just let go? Surely you would resist him and fight to hold on to it. You would strengthen your grip and refuse to let go. That's exactly what the good fight of the faith is like.

When you believe God's Word, you are holding on to His precious promise of abundant and long life. If you have His promise, you have His life; but if you let go of the promise (if you stop believing it and trusting in it), then you lose your connection to that life, so it cannot be fulfilled in your life.

Realizing this, what will you do when the enemy comes and whispers in your ear, *"That does not belong to you. Let it go. You are not worthy to have that. Look at all your sins and failures. You can't expect God to fulfill that promise for you. It will never happen to you. Don't fight me. It is easier just to let it go and see what happens. Whatever will be, will be"*? If you start listening to him, you will start to become limp and spiritually passive, and you will let go of your promise from God.

Many Christians are wimps when it comes to this fight of faith. They initially believe a promise, such as long life, and then satan comes and puts a bit a pressure on them, and tries to pull it from them, and the Christian then quickly lets go of the Word, saying, "I guess that promise is not for me." Satan comes in many disguises and uses different wiles to confuse, pressure, or persuade us to let go of God's promise. He may disguise himself as God's voice speaking through religious false teachings and unbelief that are so widespread today, such as: *"Whatever happens, good or bad, is God's will, just passively accept it. God may not want you to be healed, He wants you sick so He can teach you something."*

Satan may also try and pressure you through contradictory circumstances and afflictions to let go of the Word, or he may try and distract you from the Word with other things (the cares, pleasures, needs, and responsibilities of life) to cause you to loosen your grip (see the Parable of the Sower). His strategy is to feed you his unbelief to paralyze your faith, causing you to doubt in your heart that the promise is for you, for then you will let it go, and he will have won, for that Word of God can no longer produce good fruit for you. To doubt means having a divided mind that is no longer sure if God's Word is true. It also means to differ with the Word.

If you don't know how to fight the good fight of the faith, satan will sucker you into doubt and defeat every time. God gives us His Word that promises us long life, but there is a battle over whether we believe it or not (a fight of faith). The basic issue is, do we believe God's Word or satan's lies? When satan comes to steal the Word from us, we should recognize him with his wiles and lies and be ready for him. When he tries to make us lessen our grip and take the Word from us, we must quickly respond by laying hold of the Word of God all the more and by resisting satan.

How do we do this? By affirming, declaring, and confessing the Word, saying, "The promise is mine. It belongs to me in Christ." Then when he can see that you are fully persuaded by God's Word and fully resolved to believe it so that he is wasting his time, he will leave you: "Submit to God [and His Word]. Resist the devil [and his unbelief] and [then] he will flee from you" (James 4:7).

First Timothy 6:12 proves that the good fight of the faith involves laying hold by faith of God's life, and we do this by laying hold of God's promise (Word) of life. Effort is needed, because contrary pressures and persuasions will come from the world, the flesh, and the devil to let it go. We need a bulldog faith that holds on to the Word with a death-defying grip that refuses to let go no matter what.

How can we fight this good fight and defeat satan every time? Jesus showed us the way. He gave us His example to follow. When He was tempted by satan in the wilderness three times (see Matthew 4), He used the same method every time to fight the fight of faith and defeat satan. He only used one method to resist satan and make him flee—He used the *Word of God*! He spoke the Word of God; each time He opened His mouth saying, "It is written" (Matthew 4:4,7,10). He said nothing else to satan apart from the Word, and then He commanded him to be gone! Then the devil left him (Matthew 4:11).

Our victory in this warfare is through the Word of God, not by our strength or personality or IQ. We are foolish if we try and argue with the devil or outwit him. If we depend on ourselves we will fail. The *only way* to successfully resist satan is with the Word of God on our lips: "They overcame him [satan] by the blood of the Lamb and by the word of their testimony" (Revelation 12:11). This guarantees victory.

If Jesus had to speak the Word in order to defeat satan, then surely we do also! If there was some other way to fight, then He would have shown it to us, but He only gave us one method to use—God's Word on our lips. And we do not need any other method, because the Word works every time!

Too many Christians are passive; they accept any thought that satan puts in their minds. They think satan comes in a red outfit with a pitch-fork! No, he comes by whispering thoughts into the mind like: *"You don't believe that do you? Did God really say that? You can't take it liter-ally. God does not mean that. He does not really love you. His Word won't work for you."* Satan comes to steal from you by thoughts of failure, gloom, doubt, and fear—to stop you from trusting God.

The only way to fight him is to speak the Word. That's how Jesus defeated him. He did not argue with him. Satan flees from the Word. So *the first key to winning the fight* of faith *is to know and understand the Word*; otherwise, we have automatically lost. We must know what is written. Our essential preparation is to study the promises and know they belong to us. We must establish the Word in our lives. When we know the promise, then we can embrace it for ourselves (believe we receive it), saying, "It's mine; I take it now." This is possessing, claiming, and taking hold of the promise for ourselves. We must receive the Word into us.

We have to make it ours and be ready to keep hold of it.

Satan will come to test our faith in the Word, but if we wrap ourselves firmly in the promise of God, it will hold us firm in the battle. The fight for our lives is won or lost in our minds, so when evil thoughts of unbelief come, we must not dwell on them or be passive and let them have a place in us. Instead, we must immediately take action and put the Word (promise) on our lips and speak it with confidence, thus nullifying and breaking the power of those thoughts over us. When we speak the Word, we not only dismiss the doubts but also affirm and establish our faith, strengthening our hold on the promise.

First Timothy 6:12 says, "Fight the good fight of [the] faith, lay hold on eternal life, to which you are also called, and have confessed a good confession in the presence of many witnesses." Paul tells us to fight the fight of the faith (the Word), and then he tells us how to fight this fight. First, we are to lay hold of God's life by taking hold of His Word (claiming His promise) on the basis that it belongs to us, for as His children we are called of God to possess His life. Then when we come under pressure and attack to let it go, we must confess the Word with boldness and accuracy. In this way, we will fight a good fight, keep hold of the promise of life, and enjoy the victory (the promise manifested).

Declare:

> To the thought: "There's too much opposition," we must say, "It is written: 'No weapon formed against me shall prosper, and every tongue which rises against me in judgment I shall condemn. This is the heritage of the servants of the LORD, and their righteousness is from God'" (see Isaiah 54:17).

> To the thought: "I am not loved by God," we must say, "It is written: 'God loves me with an everlasting love. God desires that I prosper and be in health even as my soul prospers'" (see Jeremiah 31:3; 3 John 2).

To condemnation, we say: "It is written: 'There is no condemnation for those who are in Christ Jesus. I am a new creation in Christ, old things are passed away...Jesus, who knew no sin, became sin for me, so I might become the righteousness of God in Christ'" (see Romans 8:1; 2 Corinthians 5:17,21).

To curses we must say: "It is written: 'I have been blessed with every spiritual blessing in Christ. Christ has redeemed me from the curse, having become a curse for me, for cursed is everyone who hangs on a tree that the blessing might come upon me'" (see Ephesians 1:3; Galatians 3:13-14).

To the thought: "God won't forgive me," we are to say: "It is written: 'If we confess our sins, He is faithful (to His Word) and just (through the blood) to forgive us our sins and cleanse us from all unrighteousness'" (see 1 John 1:9).

To sickness we say: "It is written: 'He forgives all my sins and heals all my diseases. He Himself bore my sicknesses and carried my pains, by His stripes I am healed'" (see Psalm 103:3; Isaiah 53:4-5; Matthew 8:17; 1 Peter 2:24).

To fears, we say: "It is written: 'God has not given me a spirit of fear but of power, love and a sound mind. I shall not fear, for You Lord are with me. You will never leave or forsake me, so I will boldly say, "the Lord is my helper, I will not fear. What can man do to me?"'" (see 2 Timothy 1:7; Psalm 23:4; Isaiah 41:10; Hebrews 13:5-6).

To "You will have a short life" say, "It is written: 'I shall not die (young), but live (long) and declare the works of the LORD. With long life God will satisfy me and show me His salvation'" (see Psalm 118:17; Psalm 91:16).

Our attitude in the fight should be: God said it, I believe it, and that settles it. We fight for our lives by using our tongues to speak the words of God that cancel the power of darkness. This is how we win our spiritual battles—with God's Word. Jesus has won the victory, so we do not have to win it again. He defeated satan and established the New Covenant for us which is written in His Word and includes victory over all the power of satan. We stand in His victory, and just enforce it in our lives by declaring what is written. This puts us in the arena of faith where we automatically overcome satan.

As with any promise of God, in order to enjoy the promise of long life, we must possess it by faith, and this involves a fight of faith. God gave us a wonderful picture of this in Israel's possessing of her Promised Land of blessing.

POSSESSING OUR PROMISED LAND

We have a promised land of blessings in Christ, including long life. Just like Israel, we have to possess it by believing the Word of God and fighting the fight of faith. At the first attempt, Israel failed to enter and possess it because of unbelief, for they had not established the Word (promise) in their hearts. As a result, when they saw the enemy (the giants) they quickly forgot and let go of the promise and so failed to enter in.

Then when they had a second chance, in Deuteronomy and Joshua 1, God first gave them clear descriptions of the land, its boundaries and blessings so they knew exactly what belonged to them, with instructions on how to go in and possess it (see Deuteronomy 1:7, 11:8-31; Joshua 1:4). Then He told them the land was their inheritance from God, that it was already theirs by Covenant, that He had already given it to them, so that it was theirs for the taking—but it was up to them to go in and possess it: "See, I have set the land before you; go in and possess the land which the Lord swore [by Covenant] to your fathers...to give to them and their descendents after them" (see Deuteronomy 1:8).

Again and again God told them that they must possess the land (see Deuteronomy 11:8,10-11,23,29,31; Joshua 1:11). "For you will cross over Jordan and go in to *possess* the land which the LORD your God is giving you, and you shall *possess it and dwell* [live] in it" (Deuteronomy 11:31).

Again in Joshua 1, God said He was giving them the land, but they still had to arise, go over the Jordan, and take it by force:

> ...Now therefore arise, go over this Jordan, you and all this peo-
> ple, to the land which I am giving to them—the children of Is-
> rael. Every place that the sole of your foot will tread upon I have
> given you (Joshua 1:2-3).

They still had to go in and possess (claim) it, by putting their foot on it: "You will cross over this Jordan, to go in to possess the land which the LORD your God is giving you to *possess*" (Joshua 1:11). To give them every confidence that they had the right and the ability to claim and take the land, He told them that: 1) He had given it to them positionally (by Covenant right), and 2) He was giving it to them experientially (as they put their feet upon it by faith, He was releasing it to them).

Referring to the previous example about the big box of chocolates that you bought for your family telling them it was theirs to possess—it already belonged to them when you gave them your word (promise) that it was your gift to them. Now they can come to you anytime and take whatever they want. In one sense you have already given it to them, even before they come and claim it. Then, when they come for a piece of chocolate, you hand it over to them for them to possess. So in another sense you give it to them when they come in faith (believing your promise to them) claiming what's theirs.

Although God had already given Israel the land by means of a covenant promise (see Joshua 1:3) based upon a covenant oath, it was not theirs in experience until they believed the promise and went in to possess it. Then as they claimed in faith each piece of land by putting the soles of their feet upon it, God gave it over to them. He gave them whatever they dared to put their feet upon, because it was already theirs, waiting to be claimed. So God was giving it over to them as they were going in to possess it.

Likewise God has already given us a Promised Land of many covenant promises that are ours through the blood of Jesus. But we *must possess* our Promised Land. We have to do the possessing! It is already ours positionally, but we have to make it ours in experience by believing and claiming the promise by faith (putting our feet upon it, saying, *"It is mine; I believe; I receive it now"*). As we claim each promised blessing, it becomes ours as God freely releases (gives) it to us.

What if Joshua just waited on the edge of the land waiting for God to do something? Passive Christians say, "If God wants me to be blessed, He will just do it." No! It is ours, but we have to take it! It is ours, but we must possess it. It is up to us how much land we take. God gives us an open invitation: "Every place that the sole of your foot treads upon, I have given you" (Joshua 1:3). "Every place on which the sole of your foot treads shall be yours" (Deuteronomy 11:24). We do it one step (promise) at a time—every step a step of faith. Put your foot on the promises. Possess your possessions. God promises you that every place you put the sole of your foot shall be yours.

When you go in to possess the land, you will meet resistance. Israel had to face giants and other enemies who tried to get them off the land. Having taken some ground they had to be ready also to stand firm and hold it against enemy pressure and attack. Likewise we need the faith to lay hold of the promise, and then to keep hold of it. We must take the land and then abide in it, refusing to move from our position of faith, whatever satan tries to try and get us to let go of it.

So the main preparation needed to be successful in possessing and keeping (abiding in) the land is to be *strong in faith*. Again and again God told Joshua: "Be strong and of good courage" (see Joshua 1:6-9). Be strong means be strong in faith. The key to being strong in faith (and so to be able to go in and possess the promised inheritance) is continual meditation in the Word of God so that you know it and believe it and receive it for yourself:

> *This Book of the Law shall not depart from your mouth, but you shall meditate in it day and night, that you may observe to do according to all that is written in it. For then you will make your way prosperous, and then you will have good success* [in possessing your Promised Land] (Joshua 1:8).

Likewise we need to study God's Word so that we know our inheritance in Christ that has been freely given to us, and so that we will have the faith to go in and possess (claim) it.

This truth is also spelled out in Deuteronomy 11:8-9:

> *Therefore you shall keep every commandment which I command you today, that you may be strong* [in faith], *and go in and possess the land which you cross over to possess, and that you may prolong your days in the land which the LORD swore to give your fathers, to them and their descendants, "a land flowing with milk and honey."*

In Deuteronomy 11:18-20, He tells us to put God's Word first and establish it in our hearts: "that your days and the days of your children may be multiplied in the Land of which the Lord swore to your fathers to give them, like the days of the heavens above the earth" (Deuteronomy 11:21). He also promises that if we keep God's Word strong in us, then we will be able to take the whole land and no one will be able to stand against us, for any enemy that comes against us to remove us from the land will be defeated and will flee from us (see Deuteronomy 11:22-25).

STEPS TO POSSESSING OUR PROMISED LAND

So there are three steps to taking any part of our Promised Land:

1. We must *know* what is our Promised Land. We must find out from God's Word what He has given to us and so what belongs to us. Find the promises that cover our needs. In particular we must know that God's promise of long life is part of our inheritance, waiting to be claimed by us.

2. Then we must go in and take, *possess*, the land by faith. We plant the flag of our faith and claim what is ours—we can only claim what we know God has promised us. We put our foot on the promise, believing we receive it according to Mark 11:24. We obtain it according to Hebrews 4:16.

3. Then we *stand* firm on the promise and refuse to let satan move us off it. We must *abide* in our land. If you took possession of a house and someone challenged you and tried to remove you from it, you would take a stand and show them the title deed, where *it is written* that it is yours. Likewise we are to take the Word and declare the promise, saying, "It is written!" and command the enemy to be removed (see Revelation 12:11; Mark 11:23; Matthew 4:10).

We have the authority to do this. No mountain or giant that contradicts God's Word (trying to intimidate us so we believe in its power above God's Word) will be able to stand before us.

Stand against satan's wiles when he tries to make you doubt God's Word and persuade you that it is not working. The Christian fight is centered on believing and speaking the Word of God. Without the Word, we automatically lose. Satan's purpose is to separate us from God (and His Word), so then we are no threat and are wide open to his deception and attacks. With the Word in our heart and on our lips we win every time. By meditating and holding on to the Word, we will possess our land of promises. We abide in our possession by confession. It is a battle over the Word, so the only way to win when attacked is by holding strongly to it and declaring with our lips, *"It is written."* Retaliate by launching the Word at the enemy. Thus the attack will not only fail, but it will serve to drive you closer to God and make you more established in His Word. Then satan will flee, having lost.

Ephesians 6:10-17 instructs us how to take our stand and hold our ground when under enemy attack:

> *Finally, my brethren, be strong in the Lord and in the power of His might. Put on the whole armor of God, that you may be able to stand against the wiles* [and lies] *of the devil. For we do not wrestle against flesh and blood, but against principalities, against powers... Therefore take up the whole armor of God, that you may be able to withstand in the evil day* [of attack], *and having done all, to stand* [firm in faith]. *Stand therefore, having girded your waist with* [the belt of] *truth...and* [take] *the sword of the Spirit, which is the word* [rhema, the spoken word] *of God.*

The first and foundational piece of the armor we must put on in order to stand is the *belt* of Truth. This represents the written Word (logos). We must wrap each promise around us, by meditating on it and then by believing we receive it. The *sword* of the Spirit is placed in the belt and is to be brought forth from the belt when needed. The sword is the *rhema* or spoken word of God, which we bring forth from our knowledge of God's promises (the belt) by speaking it. Thus when we are under attack we can take the sword of the Spirit out of our belts to use against the enemy. In other words, we take an appropriate promise out from the belt of truth and speak it forth saying, "It is written," and by the Spirit it becomes a sword that cuts the enemy, for the power of the Spirit goes forth with the spoken word of God. Thus we stab satan with the sword of the spoken word of God.

So when you come under attack, stand your ground, pull your sword from your belt, and run the devil off! Thus it is through faith and patience that we receive our inheritance (see Hebrews 6:12). First by faith we believe we receive the promise (see Mark 11:24), then we patiently continue in faith, holding firmly onto the promise by holding fast to our confession of faith (see Hebrews 4:14). "Let us hold fast the confession of our hope without wavering, for He who promised is faithful" (Hebrews 10:23).

Remembering and meditating on God's faithfulness to His promises will help us to do this. It is not presumptions to claim what God has already given. In fact it pleases Him when we take Him at His Word and press in to possess our Promised Land. He said that as we do this, He would be with us to help us succeed in this task:

> *No man shall be able to stand before you all the days of your life... I will be with you. I will not leave you nor forsake you. Be strong* [in faith] *and of good courage* [to act]*...do not be afraid, nor be dismayed, for the Lord your God is with you wherever you go* (Joshua 1:5-6,9).

So meditate on God's faithfulness and His promises to you of long life (see Psalm 91:16), until you know them well and are fully assured that they are for you, and then lay hold of them by faith. After believing you receive the promised blessing, thank God for it and confess it as yours. This will further establish your faith in the promise and strengthen your grip on it. Then when satan comes with his doubts to persuade you to let it go, say, "It is written" and declare the promise!

Revelation 12:11 says, "They overcame him [satan] by the blood of the Lamb and by the word of their testimony." We overcome by applying the blood of Jesus, declaring that through His blood we have been forgiven and cleansed from all sin, made righteous with His righteousness, made children of God and joint heirs with Christ and that all the promises of God are ours in Christ, including long life. We must testify with our lips that the blood of Jesus avails for us. By shedding His blood, Jesus has done His part for us to overcome satan; but in order for us to overcome him, we must stand in what God has done for us and confess it over ourselves. We must voice our agreement with God's Word. We must testify to what the Word says the blood of Jesus has done for us.

We can do this with thanksgiving: "Lord, I thank You that through Your death I have abundant life. Through the blood of Jesus, I shall be satisfied with a long and blessed life." Jesus has overcome the power of satan, sickness, and death, for us. Through the New Covenant established in His blood, all the promises of God for life and victory are ours. All His promises are soaked in His blood, and given to us with His love. But we have to know them, believe we receive them, and proclaim them as ours in the face of satan's pressures.

We fight death with our tongue, saying, "I shall not die, but live, and declare the works of the LORD" (Psalm 118:17). We fight fear by saying, "God has not given us a spirit of fear, but of power and of love and of a sound mind" (2 Timothy 1:7)

POINTS TO PONDER

1. If you believe and speak satan's lies, you give him power over you; but if you believe and speak God's Word, satan's power is nullified.

2. With the Word in your heart and on your lips, you will win every time. By meditating and holding on to the Word, you will possess your land of promises—abiding in your possession by confession.

3. After believing you receive the promised blessing, thank God for it and confess it as yours. This establishes your faith in the promise and strengthens your grip on it. When satan comes with his doubts to persuade you to let it go, say, "It is written" and declare the promise!

Chapter 8

WHY BELIEVE FOR LONG LIFE?

Why should we claim God's promise of long life? Why fight for our lives to be fully lived? I believe there are four important reasons:

1. *To be alive for the Rapture,* which is to be expected in our generation according to the signs of the times. This was Paul's blessed hope (see 1 Corinthians 15:51; 1 Thessalonians 4:15). How wonderful it would be not to suffer death but to be changed in the twinkling of an eye and then see the Lord!

2. *Long life is God's general will for us* (see Psalm 91:16). Although there is an important exception to this rule (see Appendix A: What about Martyrdom?), long life is God's general will for believers, as we have seen through all the promises (see Appendix B: Long Life Scriptures). Therefore if we seek to fulfill God's will and best for our lives, we need to believe and pray for His will to be done in our lives, which includes long life. As we trust God for His life to sustain us in health, soundness, and strength through a long life, we glorify God and are witnesses to His loving care.

In Exodus 23:25-26, God reveals His will for us: "You shall serve the Lord your God, and He will *bless* your bread and your water; and I will take sickness away from the midst of you. ...I will fulfill the [full] number of your days." His will is to bless, and His blessing is health and long life.

First Peter 3:9-10 says, "You are called to inherit a *blessing.*" What blessing are we called to inherit? If you read on, you will see it is the blessing of a long and good life: "For he who desires life, and loves to see many good days, let him refrain his tongue from evil." God gives us the choice of life or death, blessing or cursing, and He wants us to choose life!

Deuteronomy 30:19-20 says, "I have set before you life and death, blessing and cursing [notice that blessing = life and cursing = death]; therefore [you] choose [the blessing of] life, that both you and your descendants may live [long]; [God makes it clear that His will for us is life not death] that you may love the Lord your God, that you may obey His voice, and that you may cling to Him, for He is your life and the length of your days... [the blessing of life clearly includes long life]."

The blessing (life) and the curse (death) are two opposites. The blessing of God includes healing and long life. The curse includes sickness and early death (see Deuteronomy 28).

Therefore God's will for us is the blessing of healing and long life, and He proved it supremely by sending Jesus to die for us to set us free from the curse (of sickness and early death) and release us into His blessing of health and long life. Galatians 3:13-14 says,

> *Christ has redeemed us from the curse of the law, having become a curse for us (for it is written, "Cursed is everyone who hangs on a tree"), that the blessing of Abraham might come upon the Gentiles in Christ Jesus, that we might receive the promise of the Spirit through faith.*

Sickness and early death is part of the curse (see Deuteronomy 28). But according to Galatians 3:13, Christ has redeemed us from this curse, therefore He has redeemed us from sickness and early death so that we can have the promised blessing of healing and long life. Therefore His will for us is long life.

Because Jesus died for us to set us free from the curse of sickness and early death and release us into His blessing of long life, the best way to honor His sacrifice is to receive all that He has done for us, including the blessing of long life. If we reject His provision of healing and long life, we are rejecting His will for us, and we are dishonoring His sacrifice for us. He bore the curse for us; therefore, it has no right or authority over us, and by faith we can walk free from it. We believe the Word; and as we believe it and speak it and act on it (as if it were true), it will come to pass in our lives.

Declare: Christ has redeemed me from the curse of sickness and early death. I have been set free from the curse. I have been redeemed from the curse, for Jesus took the curse for me. That means I am no longer cursed. No curse can come upon me, because I am blessed. I declare myself free right now. I am redeemed, I am delivered, I am free. God's blessing of health and long life is upon me now. Thank You, Lord. Goodness and mercy will follow me all the days of my life. Thank God, I am redeemed. Thank You, Jesus, for setting me free and releasing Your life and blessing upon me.

> Jesus Christ has redeemed me,
> as He hung on that shameful tree,
> and all that is worse
> is contained in the curse,
> and Jesus has set me free.
> For sickness I have health,
> for poverty I have wealth
> for Jesus has ransomed me.

3. *Death is an enemy to be resisted.* God did not make us for death. "The last enemy that will be destroyed is death" (1 Corinthians 15:26). Christians need not fear death for Jesus has already overcome it by His resurrection; but we are to resist death by laying hold of His resurrection life that dominates death (see Romans 6:8-9). The same life (power) that transformed His body from death to life is toward (available to work in) us who believe (see Ephesians 1:19-21). First Corinthians 15 is all about our victory over physical death: "Thanks be to God, who gives us [now] the victory [over physical death] through our Lord Jesus Christ" (1 Corinthians 15:57). Since we need victory over death, it must be our enemy, and therefore we must resist death with God's help and power.

4. *We should believe for long life and resist death so that we can fulfill our mission and destiny in life.* God has a plan and purpose for our lives: "We are His workmanship, created in Christ Jesus for good works, which God prepared beforehand that we should walk in them" (Ephesians 2:10). Our life is like a long-distance race, which God has set before us to run, and He wants us to run all the way to the finish line.

> *Therefore we also, since we are surrounded by so great a cloud of witnesses, let us lay aside every weight, and the sin which*

so easily ensnares us, and let us run with endurance the race
that is set before us, looking unto Jesus [who has already run
His race]… (Hebrews 12:1-2).

In a long distance race there are times when the runner feels like
quitting before the end. He may hit a pain-barrier and feel like he cannot continue; but if he digs deeply, he will find the extra strength to
continue and push past the barrier and pick up a second wind. But if he
is not determined to complete his course and run the full race, he will
most likely give up too soon.

Likewise we have a race to run, and there will be times when it feels
hard and we are tempted to stop pressing on to the finish line and become passive and give up. If we are not resolved to endure and run our
full race, we will fail to complete the course set before us. But if we keep
our eyes on Jesus and the joy awaiting us at the end of a good race, we
will dig deeply into the resources of God available to us and be renewed
by receiving His life into our bodies to run even stronger than before.
We need to resolve to complete our course (mission) and fulfill God's
will for us. Therefore we need to believe for a long life and fight the
fight of faith to overcome death and all resistance to make this possible.

To inspire us in this, let us look at the example of Jesus, who completed His race in spite of great opposition, suffering, and pain: "Looking unto Jesus, the author and finisher of our faith, who for the joy that
was set before Him endured the cross, despising the shame [He fully
ran His race] and has sat down at the right hand of the throne of God"
(Hebrews 12:2). Many times His life was threatened by storms and
those who wanted to kill Him, but by God's help He resisted and overcame these powers of death, because as we are often told in John's
Gospel, His time (to die) had not yet come.

Likewise, we must continue to run our race and resist death until we
know we have finished our work on earth. When Jesus suffered on the
Cross unto death, it was the final part of His earthly race, and it was in
the will and timing of God. In Gethsemene, under the pressure of all
that He would have to suffer, He felt the temptation to quit and not run
His race to the end. However, He kept the vision before Him of the joy
of accomplishing His mission to save us, and that enabled Him to endure the pain, opposition, and difficulties—and He completed His race
victoriously and now cheers us on in ours.

Apostle Paul is a great example of this overcoming attitude. He said: "Fight the good fight of faith, lay hold on eternal life to which you are called and have confessed a good confession" (1 Timothy 6:12). Paul fought a good fight overcoming death by laying hold of God's strength and life, until he knew that he had finished his course. His final victorious words:

> *The time of my departure* [from this earth] *is at hand. I have fought the good fight, I have finished the race, I have kept the faith. Finally, there is laid up for me the crown of righteousness, which the Lord, the righteous Judge, will give to me on that Day, and not to me only but also to all who have loved His appearing* (2 Timothy 4:6-8).

Paul's focus and determination to complete the race and reach the finishing line is revealed in Philippians 3:12-14:

> *Not that I have already attained, or am already perfected; but I press on that I may lay hold of that for which Christ Jesus has also laid hold of me. Brethren, I do not count myself to have apprehended; but one thing I do, forgetting those things which are behind and reaching forward to those things which are ahead, I press toward the goal for the prize of the upward call of God in Christ Jesus.*

Then verse 15 tells us that his attitude is the example for us all: "Therefore let us, as many as are mature, have this mind [attitude]; and if in anything you think otherwise, God will reveal even this [passivity] to you."

Because of persecutions and attacks stirred up by satan to stop his ministry, Paul's life was in constant danger, and he came under great pressure to quit and die before he fulfilled his ministry (see 2 Corinthians 1:8-11; 11:22-28; 12:8-10). Only by constantly drawing upon God's power could he continue to live. Many times he could have chosen to quit and go to be with the Lord. It would have been much easier; but he was a fighter, so he decided to live and fulfill his course (ministry).

Paul reveals the kind of choices he faced in Philippians 1:21-25:

> *For to me, to live is Christ, and to die gain* [he had no fear of death, for even if the worst happens it is better in heaven!]. *But if I live on in the flesh, this will mean fruit from my labor;*

yet what to choose I cannot tell [he had the choice]. *For I am hard-pressed between the two, having a desire to depart and be with Christ, which is far better* [for me]. *Nevertheless to remain in the flesh is more needful for you. And being confident of this, I know that I shall remain and continue with you all for your progress and joy of faith.*

Paul was weighing in the balance the thought of living on in a fruitful ministry against accepting an early death and going to be with the Lord. Obviously he was not considering suicide! It was simply that with all the attacks upon him, if he did not fight the fight of faith, constantly trusting God to raise him up and keep him alive, it would be impossible for him to live much longer. Such were the pressures; he felt the temptation to give up the fight and go home, but then at the end of the passage, we see that he finally decides he wants to live and fulfill his ministry, so he gets into faith that he will live and not die, so that he can fulfill his life's work for God: "being confident of this, I know that I shall remain and continue [to live] with you all" [on earth].

We too must overcome death to fulfill our course and receive the reward:

Thanks be to God, who gives us the victory [over death] *through our Lord Jesus Christ. Therefore, my beloved brethren, be steadfast, immovable, always abounding in the work of the Lord, knowing that your labor is not in vain in the Lord* (1 Corinthians 15:57-58).

Paul knew when he had finished his course (see 2 Timothy 4:6-8). We only run a good race by finishing our course and completing the work He has given us. This requires us to lay hold of God's life and to fight a good fight against death, until we have fulfilled what God has called us to do.

Final victory over death is in the resurrection, but *now* God also has given us the earnest (down payment) of the Spirit (see 2 Corinthians 5:5). We can experience now a foretaste of His life swallowing up death in our physical body (2 Corinthians 5:1-5). A measure of Christ's resurrection power is available to us now. We have seen in Second Corinthians 4:7-12 that when the spirit of death pressed in upon Paul, he was able to receive the life of Jesus manifested in his body to push back the power of death until his mission was fulfilled.

Now that we have seen we should believe for long life, how do we lay hold of Christ's resurrection life for our bodies? First Corinthians 15:57 says, "Thanks be to God, who gives us [in this life] the victory [over physical death] through our Lord Jesus Christ." God gives us victory over death in the now.

This will ultimately be fulfilled at our physical resurrection. But notice he does not say God will give us the victory, he says, "God *gives* us the victory"—now. Paul believed that through the resurrection of Jesus Christ, God gives us the victory over the power of death in this life. He did not just believe it, he proclaimed it, expressing his faith by giving thanks to God for this victory over death. He thanks God for releasing resurrection life to his body, enabling him to overcome the power of death and fulfill his mission.

Likewise, by faith we must resist the spirit of death and trust God's promise to impart Christ's resurrection life to our body *now*, and then like Paul, give thanks to God in confident faith that He is doing it, saying, "Thanks be to God who gives me the victory over death through Christ." Our declarations of faith through confession of the promise and through thanksgiving that He is doing it now, activate and release our faith and the resurrection power of God to overcome death and renew our youth.

Say with faith: *"Thanks be to God who gives me the victory over death through my Lord Jesus Christ."*

Christ has redeemed us from the curse of a life cut short so that we can have the blessing of long life, through faith. Psalm 107:1-2 tells us our part: "Oh, give thanks to the Lord, for He is good! For His mercy [His covenant love and faithfulness] endures forever. Let the redeemed of the Lord *say so* [say: "I am redeemed from the curse!"], whom He has redeemed from the hand of the enemy." Christ has redeemed us from the curse, but it is up to us to activate the blessing by thanking God for it, and by *saying*, "I am redeemed from the hand of the enemy."

Claim Romans 8:11: "If the Spirit of Him who raised Jesus from the dead dwells in you, He who raised Christ from the dead will also give [resurrection] life to your mortal bodies by His Spirit who dwells in you."

Confess: "The same Spirit of Him who raised Jesus Christ from the dead dwells in me, and He shall also quicken and give life to my mortal body by His Spirit who lives in me. Thank You, Lord, for giving me that life now."

As we continually draw on God's renewing and healing power and so fulfill our years in health and long life, our lives will be a witness and demonstration of His resurrection power to the glory of God. You will have all eternity in heaven, but only a limited and relatively short time here now to make a difference—so believe for longevity and make the best use of the time you have, so you can fulfill your purpose in this life.

Confession: "The resurrection power of Christ is working in me. I will live and not die. I will live to a full age. With long life I will be satisfied. I will fight a good fight and finish my course."

POINTS TO PONDER

1. Why should you believe for long life? To be alive for the Rapture; it is God's will for you; death is an enemy to be resisted, and so you can fulfill your mission and destiny.

2. Because Jesus died to set you free from the curse of sickness and early death and release you into His blessing of long life, the best way to honor His sacrifice is to receive all that He has done for you, including the blessing of long life.

3. As you draw on God's renewing and healing power and so fulfill your years in health and long life, your life will be a witness and demonstration of His resurrection power to the glory of God. So make the best use of the time you have, so you can fulfill your purpose in this life.

Chapter 9

SIX KEYS TO LONGER LIFE

God's will is for us to have a long and full life. We discussed that the 70-80 years of Psalm 90:10 is not the general maximum life span for believers. In Psalm 91:16 God promises a long life to believers living under His blessing and protection. The true biblical measure of humankind's full potential life span is 120 years (see Genesis 6:3). This should change the way we think about ourselves. By letting God's Word on long life renew our minds, our lives will be transformed (see Romans 12:2).

The things we *believe* and *do* either shorten or lengthen our lives. The length of our lives is not preordained. We can believe and do things that will either shorten or lengthen it. When we die is not all up to God—we have a big say in it. "The fear of the Lord prolongs days, but the years of the wicked shall be shortened" (Proverbs 10:27). The two areas of right believing and right doing, involve: 1) having faith in God's promises of long life, and 2) obeying God's wisdom in our actions and lifestyle! Wisdom in living is just as needful to long life as faith.

THE SIX KEYS TO LONG LIFE

I believe there are six essential keys to long life. The first is foundational to all the rest—putting God's Word first. The next two concern our faith life—believing and speaking. Then the last three are about applying wisdom to our lives. So, let us now consider the positive things we can believe and do in order to attain a long and full life.

Key 1. Put the Word of God First in Your Life

This key is foundational to everything, for God's Word is the source of faith and wisdom for our lives, enabling us to both believe right and live right and so lengthen our lives. God's life is in His Word, and so as we feed on it we are feeding on His life and strength. Humankind is designed to run on the spiritual fuel of God's Word: "Man shall not live by bread alone, but by every word that proceeds from the mouth of God" (Matthew 4:4). When we are not constantly taking in the Word, we run on bad fuel that leads to a shortened life (like a car working on inferior fuel). Living on good fuel brings long life. Cells in culture live long when well-nourished. Likewise, staying nourished by God's Word is the first key to long life. Again and again God promises us that if we put His Word first, it will increase the quality and quantity of our lives.

God's Word will give us a long life of many good days. Deuteronomy 11:18-21 says:

> *You shall lay up these words of mine in your heart and in your soul, and bind them as a sign on your hand, and they shall be as frontlets between your eyes. You shall teach them to your children, speaking of them when you sit in your house, when you walk by the way, when you lie down, and when you rise up. And you shall write them on the doorposts of your house and on your gates, that your days and the days of your children may be multiplied in the land of which the Lord swore to your fathers to give them, like the days of the heavens above the earth* [literally: days of heaven on earth].

Proverbs 3:1-2 says, "My son, do not forget my law, but let your heart keep my commands; for length of days, and long life and peace, they [God's words] will add to you." When you receive the wisdom in God's Word, this divine wisdom in your heart will lengthen your days.

Consider:

- Proverbs 3:13-18: "Happy is the man who finds wisdom [in the Word], and the man who gains understanding; for her proceeds are better than the profits of silver, and her gain than fine gold. She is more precious than rubies, and all the things you may desire cannot compare with her. *Length of days* is in her right hand. In her left hand riches and honor.

Her ways are ways of pleasantness, and all her paths are peace. She is a *tree of life* to those who take hold of her, and happy are all who retain her."

- Proverbs 8:35-36: "Whoever finds me [the wisdom of God's Word] finds *life*...but he who sins against me wrongs his own soul; all they who hate me love death."

- Proverbs 9:10-11: "The fear of the LORD is the beginning of wisdom, and the knowledge of the Holy One is understanding. For by me [by God's Word in you] your days will be multiplied, and years of life will be added to you."

- *God's Words are life* to our spirits, souls, and bodies; but for them to be effective, we must get and keep them in our hearts.

- Proverbs 4:4-6: "Let your heart retain my words; keep my commands, and *live*. Get wisdom! Get understanding! ...Do not forsake her, and she will *preserve* you; love her and she will keep you."

- Proverbs 4:10: "Hear, my son, and receive my *sayings*, and the years of your life will be many."

- Proverbs 4:13: "Take firm hold of instruction [the Word], do not let go; keep her, for she is your life."

- Proverbs 7:1-2: "My son, keep My words, and treasure my commands within you. Keep my commands and *live*, and my law as the apple of your eye."

- Proverbs 4:20-23: "My son, attend to my *words*; incline your ear to my *sayings*. Do not let them [the words of God] depart from your eyes; keep them in the midst of your heart. For they are *life* to those that find them, and *health* to all their flesh. Keep [protect] your heart with all diligence [by putting the Word of God first], for out of it [the heart] spring the issues [forces] of life" (sustaining us).

Our whole life and health is sustained by the strength (life) that comes out of our hearts and spirits (see Proverbs 18:14), so we need to diligently feed it with God's Word, which imparts His life to our hearts, which then issues forth from there to our minds and bodies, giving us soundness of mind and health. God's Word in our hearts also keep it strong in wisdom and faith, and guards (protects) it from foolishness and unbelief.

Third John 1:2-4 is a prayer inspired by the Spirit of God:

> *Beloved, I pray that you may prosper in all things and be in health* [God's will for us is health and long life], *just as your soul prospers* [in God's Word, which is truth, see John 17:17]. *For I rejoiced greatly when brethren came and testified of the truth* [the Word] *that is in you, just as you walk in the truth* [the Word]. *I have no greater joy than to hear that my children walk in truth* [the Word].

Divine health is God's will for us, but it is not automatic. It is according to the prosperity of our soul (mind), which depends on how much it is filled with and controlled by God's Word. If the *truth of the Word is in us and we walk in it,* then our souls will prosper; and as a result, we will prosper in all things and enjoy health and a longer life.

Second Peter 1:3-4 says:

> *His divine power has given to us all things that pertain to life and godliness, through the knowledge of Him who called us by glory and virtue, by which have been given to us exceedingly great and precious promises, that through these you may be partakers of the divine nature* [His life and health]....

In Christ, God has already given us abundant and long life. But we still have to receive (partake of) His gift by faith. It is through the promises (words) of God that we gain the knowledge of God's will and so obtain the faith we need to receive His life. Thus as we put His Word first, we come to the knowledge that God has given us all we need, and this gives us the confidence to come to Him and partake (receive).

So first we must meditate on God's Word until we *know* the promise of long life and believe it. Then on the basis of the promise, we can come to Him in confident prayer and partake of (believe we receive) that life for ourselves (see Mark 11:24). This next step is the subject of Key 2.

Key 2. Believing Prayer

The blessings of God do not come upon us automatically, for we must receive them by faith. Faith begins when the will of God is known. We come to know God's will from His Word. His Word tells us He wants us to have long life and days of heaven on earth. Once we know God's will for us, then we must embrace (believe we receive) it for ourselves, praying that His will (a long, blessed life) be done on earth (in our lives) as it is in heaven. If we want abundant life, long life, and eternal life from God, we must come to Him and ask for them:

Psalm 21:4: "He asked *life* from You, and You gave it to him—*length of days* forever and ever."

James 4:2 says we have not, because we ask not. But to ask successfully and receive it, we must ask in faith. James 1:5-7 says:

If any of you lacks wisdom [or life], *let him ask of God, who gives to all liberally and without reproach* [not withholding the answer] *and it* [life] *will be given to him. But let him ask in faith* [believing that God gives to all freely, liberally, without holding back] *with no doubting* [that God is a liberal giver who gives it to him when he asks], *for he who doubts is like a wave of the sea driven and tossed by the wind. For let not that man* [who doubts] *suppose he will receive anything from the Lord* [the Lord still gives it, but he is unable to receive it].

To ask in faith means to come to God, and to ask and receive it, trusting His promise that it is already ours in Christ, bought and paid for by His blood, and so it is freely available to us upon request. Knowing He freely gives it to us when we ask, we can come boldly to His throne of Grace to obtain it.

Consider:

- Hebrews 4:16: "Let us therefore come boldly [in confident faith that He wants to answer us and that He will freely give life to us] to the throne of *grace*, that we may *obtain mercy* and find grace to help in time of need."

- Romans 10:12-13: "…The same Lord over all is *rich* [gives freely] *to all* who call upon Him [who ask Him for life]. For 'whoever calls on the name of the Lord [Jesus], shall be saved'" [all who ask in faith shall receive His life].

- Mark 11:24: "Therefore I say to you, whatever things you desire [such as long life], when you pray, believe that you receive them [long life], and you will have them."

If you know it is God's will to have long life and that He freely gives it to us when we ask Him, we can come to Him and pray the prayer of faith and believe we receive it when we pray. Then the answer shall be manifested in our lives.

First John 5:14-15 gives the basis for us praying Mark 11:24:

Now this is the confidence that we have in Him [in His character], *that if we ask anything according to His will* [His Word], *He hears* [answers] *us. And if we know that He hears* [answers] *us, whatever we ask* [according to His will], *we know that we have the petitions that we have asked of Him* [we know we received it when we prayed].

First, we must *know* (have confidence) that what we are asking for (such as long life) is according to God's will. Second, we must *know* that when we ask for something that is His will, *He hears and answers us when we pray* (He freely releases the answer to us without delay). If we know both of these truths, then we can believe we receive the answer when we pray, and know that we have the answer to our petition. Hence we can go from His throne having the answer in our hands having obtained it by our confident faith.

Matthew 7:7-11 says:

Ask [for healing and long life], and it will be given to you [when you ask]...*For everyone who asks receives* [for it is yours and God gives it to you in the Spirit when you ask. The answer is always Yes, not No or Wait, let me think about it].... *Or what man is there among you, who if his son asks for bread* [healing is the children's bread, see Matthew 15:26] *will give him a stone* [leaving him hungry, keeping him waiting for the healing he needs]? ...*If you then, being evil, know how to give good gifts to your children, how much more will your Father who is in heaven* [immediately] *give good things* [that are bought and paid for in the New Covenant in Christ] *to those who ask Him!*

These promised blessings belong to us in Christ, but we still have to ask Him for them; but when we ask, He immediately gives them to us, so at the moment we ask, we can receive.

Luke 11:9-10: "So I say to you, ask, and it will be given to you; seek, and you will find; knock, and it will be opened to you. For everyone who asks receives, and he who seeks finds, and to him who knocks it will be opened."

Matthew 21:22: "Whatever things you ask in prayer, believing [the promise that it is yours and will be freely given to you upon request] you will receive [when you pray]."

Jesus says to us, "It is done! [it is all paid for on the Cross] I am the Alpha and the Omega, the Beginning [Source] and the End. I will *give* of the fountain of the *water of life freely* to him who thirsts [asks]" (Revelation 21:6).

This water (river) of life contains abundant life and healing. It flows from the atoning sacrifice of the Lamb:

> *He showed me a pure river of water of life, clear as crystal, pro-
> ceeding from the throne of God and of the Lamb...on either side
> of the river was the tree of life...the leaves of the tree* [which re-
> ceives its life from the river] *were for the healing of the nations*
> [therefore these waters contain healing and long life]...*let him
> who thirsts* [desires life] *come. Whoever desires* [life)], *let him
> take* [receive by faith] *the water of life* [healing and long life]
> *freely* [as a free-gift] (Revelation 22:1-2,17).

All are invited to come and take (receive by faith) what has already been poured forth (given) to us through Christ. This river of life flows freely to us in the Spirit from the Father, through the Son (the sacrificial Lamb) who has risen from the dead. It represents God freely giving us His life and healing, flowing to us in and by the Spirit, on the basis of the blood of Jesus.

We have seen the first two keys of receiving long life by faith. Key 1 is to know the promise of God and be fully persuaded that it is God's will for our lives. This comes through meditating on the Word. Key 2 is the next step. On the basis of the promise, we must come to God in faith, and ask Him for what is promised, and believe we receive it.

We now come to Key 3, which completes this process of faith. It is the key to maintaining and strengthening our faith in the promise, and for bringing the answer (which we have now received into our spirits) into manifestation in our lives.

Key 3. Use Your Tongue to Speak Life and Health

We are made in the image of God, who brings forth what He has in His Spirit into physical manifestation by speaking words (see Genesis 1). So when we have received a promise of God by faith, we have the answer in our spirits. Now we are to bring it into manifestation by speaking words. As we do, we release God's Spirit to work and perform the promise (see Genesis 1:2-3; Psalm 33:6). As we confess the promise and thank God for bringing it to pass, we are activating the power of God in us and calling the answer into manifestation. At the same time we are defending our hearts against the entrance of doubt and unbelief.

Consider:

- Matthew 12:34-35: "Out of the abundance of the heart the mouth speaks [first we fill our heart with the Word, believing we receive His promises of life, then we speak life forth. Thus:] A good man out of the good treasure of his heart [the Word stored in His heart] brings forth good things [by his words of life], and [likewise] an evil man out of the evil treasure [of his heart] brings forth [by his words] evil things" [death].

- Proverbs 18:21 agrees: "Death and life are in the power of the tongue, and those who love it will eat its fruit." You will eat your words! If you speak words of death, you produce death in yourself; but if you speak life, you will release life.

- Psalm 103:5: "He satisfies [fills] your *mouth* with good things, so that *your youth is renewed* like the eagle's." If we let God feed us with His Word so that our hearts and mouths are filled with good things (such as His promises of long life), then our youth will be renewed unto long life.

First Timothy 6:12 says, "Fight the good fight of [the] faith." It goes on to tell us how to do this: 1) lay hold by faith on eternal life (the life of God) to which we were called (which therefore belongs to us in Christ), and 2) confess the good confession (of the Word). We are not to be passive in our faith, but we must fight for our life, because there is an enemy trying to take life from us by trying to get us into sin and unbelief through his deception. Don't be robbed of one day. This life is short enough anyway—so don't let it be cut even shorter. It is a fight, which means we must put forth effort to overcome opposition. It is a fight of faith, which is won by means of our faith in the Word of God.

So we must *know it, believe it, and speak it.*

It is a good fight, because we will always win it if we hold fast to the Word, for the power of the Word of God will always overcome the lies and power of the enemy. In this fight we must actively lay hold of the life of God that has been given to us, and then we are to keep a firm hold on it.

We do this by laying hold of the Word, for God's life is in His Word. Our connection to His life is through His Word. First, we are to establish our faith on the promises of God's Word, and believe we receive His (long and abundant) life. Thus, we are to lay hold of His life by firmly laying hold of (embracing) His Word (promise) to us, by faith.

Second, having laid hold of His promise of life and received it, we are then to stand our ground in faith and refuse to let go of the promise. We do this by confessing a good confession, that is, we are to make a bold confession of faith in the promise of God. When attacked by satan's lies, contrary feelings and circumstances, or other pressures to let go of the promise, we must confess God's Word over our lives. We are to speak God's Word out loud, just as Jesus did when He was under attack (see Matthew 4), by saying: "It is written," and then confess with confidence God's promises of long life.

We should take our stand and declare: "I shall not die [young], but live [long], and declare the works of the Lord" (Psalm 118:17). This will nullify satan's attack, protect your heart from his lies and unbelief, and tighten your grip on God's promise. We must fight unbelief, sickness, fear, and the spirit of death with God's Word on our lips.

If Jesus fought the fight of faith by knowing, believing, and speaking God's Word, so should we. If Jesus had to speak God's Word in the face of attack in order to defeat the enemy, then how much more is it necessary for us to do the same!

James 4:7 describes the same two-stage process of faith: "[1] Submit to God [by believing we receive His promise], then [2] resist the devil [by confessing His Word] and [as a result] he will flee from you" [in terror].

Ephesians 6:13-17 agrees. 1) We are to put on *the belt of truth*. This is knowing the Word, embracing it, wrapping it around ourselves, making it ours, believing we receive it.

Then 2) we take a specific promise out from the belt, putting it on our lips, so that it becomes *the sword of the Spirit* that cuts the enemy, causing him to flee from you.

Likewise, we saw that Second Corinthians 1:20 says we must 1) realize the promises are for us, and 2) add our Amen agreement to them if we are to see them manifested in our lives.

Hebrews 11:13 reveals the same process of faith: 1) having seen them [the promises] afar off, they were assured (persuaded) of them (they knew the promises), embraced them (they personally received them), and 2) confessed that they were strangers and pilgrims on the earth (they spoke and acted on them).

We must not only 1) believe God's promises of youth renewal and long life, we must also 2) speak them if they are to be established in our hearts and fulfilled in our lives.

These two steps of faith are also evident in how Abraham received his youth renewal. God gave Abraham a promise of youth renewal in order for him to have a son at 100 years of age. Abraham 1) believed and 2) spoke this promise of youth renewal, and it came to pass!

God gave Abraham the promise: "I have made you a father of many nations" and told him to walk before Him in fellowship, to believe Him and follow His lead (see Genesis 17:1). Romans 4:17 describes his response of faith to this promise: "...in the Presence of Him whom he believed: God, Who 1) *gives life* to the dead and 2) *calls* (speaks) those things which do not exist as though they did." 1) God gives a renewal of life to his dying body. So his first response of faith was to believe he received this new life for his body. 2) God called him Abraham, the father of many nations, before it was manifested. So, his second response of faith was to agree with God and call himself Abraham, even before it was manifested. Thus he confessed the promise as true before he saw it. By Abraham's words he called the promise forth into manifestation.

Thus God was able to bring His promise of youth renewal and long life to pass through Abraham's faith. Romans 4:18-21 describes in greater detail how Abraham received the promise, saying he 1) received strength (into his body) by faith, and 2) gave glory to God (confessing the promise and thanking God for bringing it to pass, even before he saw the answer), being fully convinced that what God had promised He was also able to perform.

Likewise, we are to walk in fellowship with God, believing and receiving His promises of youth renewal and long life and then calling them into manifestation by confessing the promises and giving glory to God for fulfilling them in us.

We have seen that in the face of death, the Messiah released His faith in the same way, for newness of resurrection life to overcome death. He declares God's promise over His life: "I will walk before the Lord in the land of the living" (Psalm 116:9). Then He explained the process of faith at work: "[1] I believed [the promise], therefore [2] I [also] spoke [the promise]" (Psalm 116:10). By speaking the word He released His faith and God's power to bring the promise to pass.

Paul, in Second Corinthians 4:13-14, refers to these verses in Psalm 116, and calls us to exercise our faith in the same way to get the same results: "Since we have the same spirit of faith [as the Messiah], according to what is written, 'I believed [the Word], and therefore I spoke' [the Word], we also believe (the Word), and therefore speak [the Word], knowing that He who raised up the Lord Jesus will also raise us up with Jesus." We are to move in the same spirit of faith as Jesus, believing and speaking life in the face of weakness, sickness, and death, knowing that just as God fulfilled His promise to Jesus to raise Him up to newness of life, so He will also fulfill His promises to us, by imparting His resurrection life to us.

The same power that raised Jesus, overcoming (reversing) death and filling Him with life is freely available to us to be received by the same kind of faith that Jesus walked in.

Romans 10:9-10: "If you *confess* with your mouth the Lord Jesus and believe in your heart that God has raised Him from the dead, you will be saved [receive the promise of life]. For [1] with the heart one *believes* [and receives the promise] unto righteousness, and [2] with the mouth *confession* [of the promise] is made unto salvation" [producing the manifestation of the promise].

Jesus described this process of faith in Mark 11:22-24. Mark 11:22 says, "Have faith in God" [literally: "have the faith of God" or "have the God-kind of faith"]. He is telling us to operate in the very same kind of faith as God did at creation that is: 1) to believe-receive it in our heart, and then 2) to speak it into manifestation with our lips (confession).

Then Jesus focused on the speaking part in Mark 11:23: "For assuredly, I say to you, whoever *says* to this mountain [whatever is blocking the promise being fulfilled] 'Be removed and be cast into the sea,' and does not doubt in his heart [literally: 'does not let doubt enter into his heart'] but believes that those things he *says* will be done [come to pass] he will have [manifested] whatever he *says*."

"He will have whatever he says," but only if he "believes that what he says will come to pass." Thus we can only successfully speak the answer forth, if we are already in faith, having believed we have received it in our spirits. This is confirmed by the requirement of not letting doubt enter our hearts. So in Mark 11:23, we have already entered the realm of having believed we have received it, but there is a danger of letting unbelief into the heart from looking at the mountain (the contradictory circumstance) that stands in the way. Therefore Mark 11:23 tells us that having believed we have received it, we must maintain our position of faith, protecting our hearts from the entrance of doubts, and speak the promise into manifestation, calling and commanding life and healing power to come into our bodies and commanding sickness to leave, believing that what we say will be done, for we will have what we say.

So, before we implement Mark 11:23 and speak the answer forth believing it will come to pass, we must know we have it in the spirit. Thus we must first of all receive it from God by faith. When God calls something forth (as at creation), He already has it in His Spirit; so likewise before we can successfully speak a promise into manifestation, we must first receive it from God into our spirit.

Therefore, after Jesus tells us how to speak words of faith in Mark 11:23, He tells us in verse 24 how to get into position to do it: "Therefore [in order to be in position to obey verse 23], I say to you, whatever things you desire [such as long life], when you pray, believe that you receive them [spiritually], and you will have them" [see them manifested physically].

Notice that "having" the answer is mentioned in both verses: "you will have them" (v24), and "he will have what he says" (v23). The first key to having them, is believing we receive them from God. The second key to having them (manifested) is speaking them forth, believing that what we say will come to pass (through God's power) for "we will have whatever we say." If we know we have received healing and long life, then we can speak it into our lives, and command sickness to be removed: "I will be satisfied with long life and health. The Lord is the strength of my life. Body, be renewed! Sickness, be gone in Jesus' name!" and we will have what we say, if we believe that our words will come to pass through the Spirit of God working with us.

Mark 11:24 says that if we believe we receive it, then we will have it, but verse 23 clarifies that this is not automatic, for it says that "we will have what we *say*." Thus "having it" does not just depend on us receiving it by faith, but also on saying (confessing) it by faith. We are only promised that we will have it, if we say it, believing that what we say will come to pass. Thus we will manifestly have what we have received by faith, if we continue in faith, calling it forth with the word of faith and commanding the removal of whatever is blocking it. Therefore to have God's promise of long life manifested in us, we must: 1) receive it from God through the prayer of faith (v24) and then, 2) speak it forth by the word of faith, also commanding any mountain in the way to be removed, believing that what we say shall come to pass (v23).

We will have what we say, if we believe it; that is, if we have believed we received it, and if we believe it is coming to pass (into manifestation) through our words. Thus, having received something through prayer, there must also be corresponding words and actions to help bring it to pass, or else God's power may become inactive through our passivity, especially if we allow doubts to enter into our hearts (about whether we really received it), turning our switch of faith off, and thus short-circuiting God's power (which is what brings the manifestation) as verse 23 warns can happen.

Thus Mark 11:23-24 describes the operation of the God-kind of faith, using reverse logic. Verse 23 says that to have the answer we must say it, believing that what we say will be done. But to do this, says verse

24, we must first believe we receive it in prayer. Thus to fulfill verse 23, we must first fulfill verse 24. Then Jesus takes this logic one step further, saying that in order to fulfill verse 24, we must first fulfill verses 25 and 26: "And whenever you stand *praying*, if you have anything against anyone, forgive him, that your Father in heaven may also forgive you your trespasses. But if you do not forgive, neither will your Father in heaven forgive your trespasses."

Unforgiveness will hinder our prayers; so in order to pray and successfully believe we receive according to verse 24, we must walk in continual forgiveness, according to verse 25. Therefore Jesus has given us step-by-step instructions on how to have God's promises come to pass in our lives through faith. Let us now summarize these steps, putting them in chronological order, by reversing the order of the verses:

- Step 1 (v25): Forgive all people as God has forgiven you.

- Step 2 (v24): Then believe you receive the answer in your spirit, basing your faith on the promise of God.

- Step 3 (v23): Then you can *speak* it forth from your spirit, believing that it will come to pass, trusting the Spirit of God to do it. You do this by *thanking* God for it, *calling* God's Life forth into manifestation, and *commanding* all opposing mountains (like sickness) to be completely removed.

So you will have the answer manifested in you, if you trust in God's promise and believe you receive it in your spirit, and then using your God-given authority you speak it into your body, for He will bring to pass what you say if you believe it. God wants to bring His Word to pass in you, but He needs your agreement (through receiving and confessing His Word) because He has given you authority (free will) over your life.

Confess: "The resurrection power of Christ is at work in me. I will live long and not die young. I will live to a full age. I will be satisfied with long life."

Key 4. The Secret to a Longer Life: Attend Church

God has made us to be part of His Church (see Matthew 16:18). God's will for all believers is to be part of a church family. Hebrews

10:25 says, "...not forsaking the assembling of ourselves together, as is the manner of some." This is healthy for us. We receive a supply of grace and spiritual cover through the fellowship of a church. "The devil walks about like a roaring lion, seeking whom he may devour" (1 Peter 5:8). A lion hunts by picking off those who are separated from the rest of the herd—easy pickings!

Regular churchgoing is good for our health, according to a scientific report. Scientists found that it dramatically raises our chances of living longer. The study, published in the *Journal of Health Psychology*, by U.S. psychologist, Dr. Michael McCullough found churchgoers have lower blood pressure, suffer less depression, and have stronger immune systems. A survey of 126,000 people found that regular church attendees were nearly a third more likely to live longer!

The health benefits of attending church derive from the presence of God, hearing the Word of God, the encouragement toward more healthy and moral living, the social support, and friendships formed there.

Key 5. Honor True Authorities in Your Life

Honoring true authorities is a key especially emphasized in the Bible, both in the Old Testaments (in the Ten Commandments) and in the New Testament, so it must have a special importance. The primary authority, of course, is God; fearing God is to have a reverential respect and honor for His authority. This is a major key to long life.

Consider:

- Proverbs 9:10-11: "The fear of the LORD is the beginning of wisdom, and knowledge of the Holy One is understanding. For by me [the reverential respect for God] your days will be multiplied, and years of life will be added to you."

- Proverbs 10:27: "The fear of the LORD prolongs days, but the years of the wicked shall be shortened."

Honoring God's authority includes honoring His delegated earthly authorities. The first earthly authorities we meet in life and the most important are our parents, and how we relate to them (whether we honor them or disrespect them) has a massive effect on how the rest of our life works out.

- Exodus 20:12: "Honor your father and your mother, that your days may be long upon the land which the LORD your God is giving you."

- Deuteronomy 5:16: "Honor your father and your mother, as the Lord your God has commanded you, that your days may be long, and that it may be well with you in the land which the Lord your God is giving you." This says that honoring parents is a key to good days and a long life.

This key is re-affirmed in the New Testament. Ephesians 6:2-3 says, "'Honor your father and mother,' which is the first commandment with promise: 'that it may be *well* with you and you *live long* on the earth.'"

Many have rebelled against their parents, or have bitterness and un-forgiveness toward them, and wonder why their lives are not working out well. To honor and respect your parents does not mean you always have to agree with them, but you still honor them and the place they have in your life. If you don't learn to honor the authority of your parents, then that will carry over to all your other relationships with authorities in the workplace and in society, so that your life will constantly be disrupted and not work out well.

Notice it says to honor those in authority that it may be well with us and that we live long on the earth. This implies that if we do not honor them it is impossible for things to be well with us and that we live long on the earth. Honoring authority, starting with our parents, is essential for a long life.

Discerning and submitting to true delegated authority is essential to a good long life. Rebellion tries to usurp and undermine authority, and it will shorten your life. Authority is the strongest stuff around because it derives from God, and so it has a powerful effect on how your life works out. Where you meet true authority you meet God, so the way you honor or dishonor it has a significant effect on how long and how well you live. (Any authority that overreaches its boundaries is false, and you are not then required to obey it.)

The main authorities that God has established in our lives are:

1. Free will (We must respect people's freedom of choice over their own lives and overriding that through manipulation or intimidation is a form of rebellion and witchcraft.)

2. Parents and children

3. Government authorities (police, judges, etc.)

4. Authorities in the Church

5. Authorities at work

If we fear and respect God, we will give due honor to all these authorities in our lives, even if we think they are wrong. As a result, it will be well with us, and we will live long on the earth.

Key 6. Obeying and Serving God with a Willing Heart

Consider these Scripture verses regarding Key 6:

Exodus 23:25-26 says, "You shall serve the LORD your God, and He will bless your bread and your water. And I will take sickness away from the midst of you...and I will fulfill the number of your days" [your full life-span]. "If you walk in My ways, and keep My statues and My commandments...then I will lengthen your days" (1 Kings 3:14; see Proverbs 28:16).

Isaiah 1:19 says, "If you are *willing* and *obedient*, you shall eat the good of the land" (including a long life).

The reward does not just come from being obedient, but from doing it with the right attitude of heart, being willing and obedient, serving the Lord with joy and enthusiasm, rather than as a burdensome duty. Kenneth Hagin said that when he was called to leave pastoring to go on the road as a traveling teacher, he struggled financially for the first year. When he complained that things were not going well, even though he had been obedient, the Lord gave him this Scripture from Isaiah 1 saying he had been obedient, but he had not been willing—and it is the willing *and* obedient who will eat the good of the land. He had been obeying God but only reluctantly not joyfully. Kenneth Hagin said that he quickly became willing, and then the blessings started to flow!

So truly serving and obeying God means doing His will from the heart, with the right heart attitudes and motives. This means serving Him willingly and with enthusiasm, seeking His glory. It also means walking in an attitude of *humility*.

Proverbs 22:4 says, "By humility and the fear of the Lord are riches, and honor, and [long] life." Humility includes being correctable and being able to say we are sorry. It is hard to humble ourselves, but it releases life to us (see James 4:6). Often there are faults on both sides, but we can always apologize for our part in any wrong. It takes more humility to apologize first, but it will soften the other person's heart. Pride means never saying sorry; it is a deception that we are always right, that we always know best which makes us hard and unteachable—and it will lead to a fall and early death.

Proverbs has a lot to say about this truth: "Pride goes before destruction, and a haughty spirit before a fall... There is a way that seems right to a man, but its end is the way of death" (Proverbs 16:18,25). "He who covers his sins will not prosper, but whoever confesses and forsakes them will have mercy. Happy is the man who is always reverent, but he who hardens his heart will fall into calamity" (Proverbs 28:13-14). "He who is often rebuked, and hardens his neck, will suddenly be destroyed, and that without remedy" (Proverbs 29:1).

The attitudes of heart and mind that promote long life are the very attitudes that the Holy Spirit is seeking to produce in us. Galatians 5:22-23 says, "The fruit of the Spirit is love, joy, peace, longsuffering, kindness, goodness, faithfulness, gentleness, self-control." These qualities are issuing forth from our re-born spirit which is united to the Holy Spirit, so as we walk in the Spirit the law of the Spirit of life in Christ Jesus makes me free from the law of sin and death" (see Romans 8:2). Jesus made it possible for us to experience this life of the Spirit through His death for us. He took our sin so "that the righteous requirement of the law [love] might be fulfilled in us, who do not walk according to the flesh but according to the Spirit" (see Romans 8:3-4).

We choose to walk in the Spirit by setting our minds on the things of the Spirit: "those who live according to the flesh set their minds on the things of the flesh, but those who live according to the Spirit, the things of the Spirit" (Romans 8:5). If we mind the things of the Spirit and so cultivate the fruit of the Spirit, this will result in a longer life, whereas focusing on the flesh brings death: "For to be carnally minded is *death*, but to be spiritually minded is *life* and peace" (Romans 8:6).

Two attitudes of the Spirit that lead to long life are:

1. Love—the main commandment of God means loving God with all our hearts, and loving others as ourselves, doing unto them as we would have them do unto us. This includes freely forgiving them as God in Christ has forgiven us (see Ephesians 4:32).

2. Joy—"the joy of the Lord is your strength" (Nehemiah 8:10). As you rejoice in God with praise and thanksgiving, the life and strength of God will be released into your being. Praise will silence the work of the enemy in your life (see Psalm 8:2). Proverbs 17:22 says, "A merry heart [the joy of the Lord] does good, like medicine, but a broken spirit dries the bones."

Living under a spirit of fear and depression will sap our strength and shorten our lives, but God wants to give us beauty for ashes, the oil of joy for mourning, and the garment of praise for the spirit of heaviness (see Isaiah 61:3). Proverbs 4:23 says, "Keep [Guard] your heart [from bad attitudes] with all diligence, for out of it spring the issues of [your] life."

Your life comes out from your heart, so if it is sound then your life-force will also be strong; but if bad attitudes enter your heart, they will weaken your health and shorten your life. "A sound heart is life to the body, but envy [and hatred] is rottenness to the bones" (Proverbs 14:30).

POINTS TO PONDER

1. The six keys to longer life: put the Word of God first in your life; believe you receive His promise of long life and youth renewal in prayer; speak life and health; attend church; honor authority; obey and serve God willingly.

2. God made you to be part of His Church; regular churchgoing is good for your health, dramatically raising your chances of living longer.

3. If you mind the things of the Spirit and so cultivate the fruit of the Spirit, this will result in a longer life, whereas focusing on the flesh brings death.

Chapter 10

SIX KILLERS OF LONGER LIFE

It should be obvious by now from readings throughout Scripture that God's will is for us to have a long and full life. In Psalm 91:16, God's promise to those who dwell in the secret place of the Almighty is: "With long life will I satisfy him, and show Him My salvation." In John 10:10, Jesus said that although satan comes to steal, kill, and destroy, Jesus has come to give us abundant life now, and long life, and eternal life: "The thief does not come except to steal, and to kill, and to destroy. I [Jesus] have come that they may have life, and that they may have it more abundantly."

God's promises of long life come with conditions. The promise is given to build our faith to believe and receive it, for it reveals that God's will is for us to have it. The conditions are given to impart His wisdom to us, so we know how to live and what to avoid, so that we can see the promise fulfilled in us, rather than it being aborted.

When God gives conditions, it does not mean that longevity is not really His will and so He wants to make it difficult for us to achieve, but because it is His will, He shows us how we can attain the promise and see it fulfilled in our lives. He gives His commandments so that by obeying them we can have abundant life—spiritual and physical. He tells us what to do and what to avoid, so we can have a good and long life. When He tells us not to do something, He does so because He loves us and He knows that sin will bring death into our lives and shorten our life span. His laws warn us to avoid things that will kill us and cut short our lives. For example, Proverbs 13:14 says, "The law of the wise is a fountain of life, to turn one away from the snares [traps] of death."

In this chapter, six killers are revealed through God's Word: foolishness, sin, unforgiveness, evil speech, worry, and passivity. These are snares that can cut short our lives.

KILLER 1: FOOLISHNESS

Wisdom is the skillful application of God's Word to our lives. It comes from God's Word and will lengthen our lives:

> *...Let your heart retain my words: keep my commands, and live. Get wisdom! ...Do not forsake her [wisdom], and she [wisdom] will preserve you; love her [wisdom], and she [wisdom] will keep you* (Proverbs 4:4-6).

> *By me [wisdom] your days will be multiplied, and years of life will be added to you* (Proverbs 9:11).

> *Happy [blessed] is the man who finds wisdom, Length of days is in her right hand...* (Proverbs 3:13,16).

> *Whosoever finds me [wisdom] finds life. ...But he who sins against me [wisdom] wrongs his own soul; all those who hate me love death* (Proverbs 8:35-36).

General wisdom (that applies to all people equally) comes from the Word. We also need special wisdom for specific situations we face, and this comes from the Spirit of Wisdom (the Holy Spirit) who lives within us. We are invited to ask God for His wisdom and receive it whenever we need it (see James 1:5). As we open ourselves to hear His wisdom and pray in the Spirit, it will come into our minds. We must learn to be led by the Spirit (see Romans 8:14).

Foolishness is to ignore the warnings of wisdom, by which we can avoid satan's traps and stay clear of danger. There are two main ways to die young: being overly wicked and foolish: "Be not overly [1] *wicked* [sin will shorten your life, for the wages of sin is death], nor be [2] *foolish*, why should you die before your time?" (Ecclesiastes 7:17).

Foolishness may not involve deliberate sinning, but it is always a lack of wisdom. It includes such things as eating the wrong foods, not drinking enough water, smoking, being passive, not exercising, overworking, not resting enough, and letting ourselves get stressed out too much.

Often we do not handle stress well. There are times when we are under great pressure and our mind and body adjusts to that, but we must not live in that state for a prolonged time. We must take time out of the rush of doing to *trust* God, for He will provide for us. He is the Source of your life: "I lay in Zion a stone for a foundation, a tried stone, a precious cornerstone, a sure foundation [Jesus]; whoever believes [trusts in Him] will not act hastily" (Isaiah 28:16).

Jesus said, "Come to Me, all you who labor and are heavy laden, and I will give you rest. Take My yoke upon you and learn from Me, for I am gentle and lowly in heart, and you will find rest for your souls. For My yoke is easy and My burden is light" (Matthew 11:28-30).

We need to take time out, to get the big picture, to see our lives in God's hands, and to believe that He will provide for us:

> *He gives power to the weak, and to those who have no might He increases strength...those who wait on the Lord will renew their strength; they will mount up with wings like eagles, they will run and not be weary; they will walk and not faint. Keep silence before Me...and let the people renew their strength! Let them come near...* (Isaiah 40:29–41:1).

The world will not come to an end if we stop our activity!

The Rhythm of Life

There is a rhythm of life. God has designed us to live in that rhythm. He created the days, weeks, and years. Stress will build up in our minds and bodies when we lose our rhythm. We are designed to live in cycles of activity and rest.

The daily cycle of night (rest) and day (activity) is written about in Genesis 1. In our dreams, the build-up of the day's events is discharged, and our brains are renewed to work again; good sleep is necessary for our mental and physical health. If we learn to live one day at a time (see Matthew 6:11,34; Psalm 118:24; Lamentations 3:22-23), daily receiving the grace we need for that day and not worrying about tomorrow, rejoicing in each day the Lord gives and living it to the full, then we will manage the stress and pressures of life so much better.

The weekly cycle is one that recognizes God made the world in six days and rested on the seventh day (see Genesis 1:3–2:3), establishing the week as a basic cycle of life, with the creation week being a blueprint for every week. He commanded Israel to strictly observe this pattern of life, by resting on the Sabbath (see Exodus 20:8-11; Deuteronomy 5:12-15). In correcting their legalism Jesus said, "The Sabbath was made for man, not man for the Sabbath" (Mark 2:27). Therefore, it is for our good to rest one day a week to honor God, acknowledging that He is our Creator, and so our whole life comes from Him by grace.

God gives us a day of rest from normal activities to learn that our life ultimately rests in God's grace and not our works (that's why getting legalistic over the Sabbath defeats its purpose). God gives us a day of rest to relax and focus on God, to regain perspective (by getting the big picture and rising above the details) and to thank, worship, and enjoy God.

Thus any build-up of stress and exhaustion from the week can be washed away, and we can enter the new week refreshed and renewed to work better, living out from the rest and grace of God. God made us and so He knows what is best for us. He knows what will cause us to live better and longer, and so He has given us the Sabbath principle to live by.

God designed us to live according to a weekly cycle of work and rest, and in His love God revealed this Sabbath-principle to us for our benefit; but if we abuse it, we will pay a price in the quality and quantity of our days on earth. At one point Russian Communism tried to establish a 10-day week in that country, but it led to less production and more sickness, so they were forced to return to a 7-day week—God knows best!

I believe that the loss of observing the Sabbath principle by much of our society is a big reason for increased mental problems—people have no rhythm to their lives. They don't discharge their stress properly, and they don't recharge spiritually. When they work all week and don't rest, they lose efficiency and grind themselves down to an early death. Science shows that living cells in a culture dish that are kept under constant stress (pressure) die young. Our bodies and brains can be compared to a car. If we service it regularly it will work better and have a longer life. But if we keep it running without a service, we will gradually grind it down to an early death.

We might be tempted to think we are too busy to take a day off for rest and a service (!), but this is short-sighted; for what we gain in a longer life and increased productivity through being renewed is far greater than any time we think we "lose" by stopping work for a day. Also ignoring the Sabbath rest will increasingly cause us to lose work time through increased sickness. The change of pace and focus bring us a necessary resting, refreshing, and renewing.

The Sabbath was given to Israel as a binding Law as part of the Old Covenant through Moses. The New Covenant in Christ does not make Sabbath observance a commandment in the same way (although other commandments are repeated in the New Testament, the Sabbath is not). However, the Law given to Israel is a revelation of God's character and contains important wisdom that applies to all humankind and this includes the Sabbath principle. Jesus confirmed this when He said, "The Sabbath was made for man" (Mark 2:27), and that He was the "Lord of the Sabbath" (Mark 2:28).

Therefore, whatever our working patterns and routines are, if we want to walk in wisdom and honor God as our Creator, we will endeavor to implement the Sabbath principle into our way of life as best we can, whether it is Saturday, Sunday, or some other day. To ignore God's wisdom is foolishness, and ultimately it will shorten our lives, for without a weekly renewal we will wear out sooner.

Foolishness can also be ignoring warnings of the Spirit. Often we can get too busy to pray and meditate in God's Word, so we fail to dwell under the shadow (protection) of the Almighty as we ought (more about this in Chapter 11). This makes us more vulnerable to sickness and means we fail to hear God when He warns us about danger and wants to guide us around it. Ministers, especially when they become successful, can fall into this trap, putting their ministry before their relationship with God.

KILLER 2: SIN

As mentioned previously, Ecclesiastes 7:17 points out the two main ways to die young: being overly wicked and foolish. "Be not overly wicked, nor be foolish: why should you die before your time?" In the prior sections, we discussed the dangers of foolishness; now we will point out that sin (wickedness) will surely shorten your life, for "The wages of sin is death" (Romans 6:23). Sin always leads to death. This is the law of sin and death (see Romans 8:2)

> *But each one is tempted when he is drawn away by his own desires and enticed. Then, when desire has conceived, it gives birth to sin; and sin, when it is full-grown, brings forth death* (James 1:14-15).

Various Scriptures tell us that violent men, deceivers (Psalm 55:23; Proverbs 28:17); thieves (Proverbs 1:18-19); adulterers (Proverbs 2:18-19; 5:3-5; 7:22-27; 9:18) will see their lives cut short. For example, First Corinthians 6:18 says, "Flee fornication. Every sin a man does is outside the body; but he who commits sexual immorality sins against his own body."

We must understand clearly that sin *always* leads to death, for it has been one of satan's main deceptions from the beginning to deny this truth, in order to encourage us to sin. In Genesis 2:17, God said, "of the tree of the knowledge of good and evil you shall not eat, for in the day that you eat of it [the day you disobey and sin] you shall surely die." God specifically warned them that sin will lead to death.

In Genesis 3:2-4 satan tried to get them to question this truth: "The woman said to the serpent [satan], "We may eat the fruit of the trees of the garden; but of the fruit of the tree which is in the midst of the garden, God has said, 'You shall not eat it, nor shall you touch it, lest you die.'" Then the serpent said to the woman, 'You will *not* surely die.'"

He tried fooling them into believing that sin has no serious negative consequences—that we can sin and get away with it. He even went one step further and said it would do them good, increasing their experience and developing their potential (see Genesis 3:5)! However they soon found out that it was all a lie, and their sin had opened the door to disease, destruction, and death. Satan still tries the same deception on each of us today! The truth of God stands firm: "The wages of sin is death."

On the other hand, just as surely as sin leads to death, righteousness leads to life: "In the way of righteousness is life, and...no death" (Proverbs 12:28). Proverbs 21:21 says, "He who follows righteousness and mercy finds life, righteousness, and honor." Proverbs 28:16 says, "A ruler who lacks understanding is a great oppressor, but he who hates covetousness will prolong his days." And Deuteronomy 25:15 says, "You shall have a perfect and just [righteous] weight, a perfect and just measure, that your days may be lengthened in the land, which the Lord your God is giving you."

Sin and righteousness are opposites leading to opposite results—death and life. Proverbs has this to say about righteousness:

- Proverbs 11:19: "As righteousness leads to life, so he who pursues evil to his own death."

- Proverbs 10:27: "The fear of the Lord prolongs days, but the years of the wicked will be shortened."

- Proverbs 24:16: "A righteous man may fall seven times and rise again, but the wicked shall fall by calamity."

A righteous man can lay hold of God's grace to rise again after falling, but sin spoils a man's ability to rebound from setbacks. So a wicked man's life will often be cut short, for he is in greater danger of not recovering when knocked down.

The length of our lives depends to a great extent on our choices as to whether or not we trust in God's grace, walk in His ways, and heed His warnings. As He says in Deuteronomy 30:19-20:

I call heaven and earth as witnesses today against you, that I have set before you life and death, blessing and cursing; therefore choose life, that both you and your descendants may live; that you may love the Lord your God, that you may obey His voice, and that you may cling to Him, for He is your life and the length of your days....

He is our life, so the more we cling to Him and His ways, the more we will receive His blessing of life and protection from the curse (death). Thus we choose life (blessing) by choosing to trust and depend on God for every area of our lives. We choose death (curse), on the other hand, by choosing to live in sin, which is going our own way in pride and independence from God, trusting in ourselves instead of God, and living in separation from God who is life (see Jeremiah 17:5-8).

Sin kills you in various ways. It cuts you off from the life of God so that you lose your joy (spiritual strength). It weighs you down with guilt and takes away your peace. It disrupts your relationships and the whole course of your life, causing an increase in stress. It gives satan (death) ground in your life.

Therefore it is essential that we quickly repent and confess our sin to God, and He will then freely forgive and cleanse us: "If we confess our sins, He is faithful and just to forgive us our sins and to cleanse us from all unrighteousness" (1 John 1:9). We must keep a short account with God.

In Psalm 32:1-5, David tells of his experience after sinning with Bathsheba. For a few months he hid his sin, and his mind and body suffered as a result, causing him to age rapidly. Then finally he confessed his sin and found the blessedness of forgiveness:

> *Blessed is he whose transgression is forgiven, whose sin is covered. Blessed is the man to whom the Lord does not impute iniquity, and in whose spirit there is no deceit* [when he no longer covers up his sin]. *When I kept silent* [when he did not confess his sin], *my bones grew old through my groaning all the day long.* [David aged quickly in this state and lost many years of life; cf Psalm 51:8.] *For day and night Your hand was heavy upon me; My vitality was turned into the drought of summer. Selah.* [Finally] *I acknowledged my sin to You, and my iniquity I have not hidden. I said, "I will confess my transgressions to the Lord," and You forgave the iniquity of my sin. Selah.*

David's sin opened the door to many major problems with his sons (see 2 Samuel 12:10-12). The stress of these combined with his premature aging caused by his unconfessed sin explains why David (a great man of God) only lived until he was 70.

Proverbs 28:13 says, "He who covers his sins will not prosper [live long], but whoever confesses and forsakes them will have mercy" [healing, renewal of life, and restoration]. And First Corinthians 11:30-31 says, "For this reason [unconfessed sin] many are weak and sick among you, and many sleep. For if we would judge ourselves, we would not be judged."

When we sin, we should judge ourselves and confess our sin to God. This will close the door on satan. But if we do not confess our sin we lose our connection to the life of God and so open the door to sickness, physical weakness, and even early death ("sleep" here is a term used for the death of a believer). Paul clearly says that unconfessed sin is a cause for Christians to be sick and to die early, but if they would judge themselves and confess their sin, they could receive forgiveness and healing and prevent their lives from being cut short (see also James 5:14-16). We all sin, but if we are quick to repent and confess it, then it will have no power to kill us.

KILLER 3: UNFORGIVENESS

Jesus included forgiveness in the Lord's Prayer—forgive us our sins, as we forgive those who sin against us (see Matthew 6:12). After giving the prayer He emphasized the importance of forgiveness: "For if you forgive men their trespasses [sins], your heavenly Father will also forgive you. But if you do not forgive men their trespasses, neither will your Father forgive your trespasses" (v14-15). You only hurt yourself when you do not forgive, not the person you are trying to punish. If you refuse to forgive, then your sins will stay upon you and they will have power over you to bring you death. The answer to your prayers (God's flow of grace and life to you) is impeded by the presence of your unforgiven sins, so you come under the dominion of the law of sin and death (see Romans 8:2).

The same warning is given after the prayer of faith in Mark 11:24: "Whenever you stand praying, if you have anything against anyone, forgive him, that your Father in heaven may also forgive you your trespasses. But if you do not forgive, neither will your Father in heaven forgive your trespasses" (Mark 11:25-26).

This is further emphasized in a parable in Matthew 18:21-35. The King (representing God) had forgiven a man's debt of millions of pounds, but then that man (representing us) refused to forgive another man of just 20 pounds. When the king heard about this, he "was angry, and delivered him to the torturers until he should pay all that was due to him. So My heavenly Father will also do to you if each of you, from your hearts, does not forgive his brother his trespasses [sins]" (Matthew 18:34-35). God has forgiven us so much, and if we do not forgive others, our past sins come back on us and have power over us to bring death (we open the door to satan, and give him the right to torment and hurt us).

Forgiveness is especially important with those close to us for they are most likely to upset us. Do not let barriers of cold anger and resentment build up. We must also forgive ourselves once we have confessed our sin with proper contrition. Blaming God for something is also a form of unforgiveness.

So, walking in daily forgiveness is a major key to long life. It is a decision—not a feeling. We are to forgive freely and completely, just as God has forgiven us (see Ephesians 4:32). When God forgives us He forgets (see Jeremiah 31:34, Hebrews 8:12). He does not bring it up again to His conscious mind. To test if you have truly forgiven, ask yourself, "Can I pray for the person? Am I always bringing up their sin? Do I interpret everything they do in a negative light?"

KILLER 4: EVIL SPEECH

We have seen how speaking God's words releases life and blessing to us, but words can also be containers of death. Evil speech about God, ourselves, or others will bring us death. Consider what the Bible says about this topic:

- Proverbs 18:21: "Death and life are in the power of the tongue, and those who love it shall eat its fruit" [death or life]. You will eat the fruit of your own tongue. Words contain the power of life or death. If you speak evil and death, those empowered words go into you (you literally eat your words!).

- Psalm 109:17-19: "As he loved cursing, so let it come to him; as he did not delight in blessing, so let it be far from him. As he clothed himself with cursing as with his garment, so let it enter his body like water, and like oil into his bones. Let it be to him like the garment which covers him, and for a belt with which he girds himself continually."

- Proverbs 15:4: "A wholesome tongue is a tree of life, but perverseness in it breaks the spirit."

- Proverbs 13:3: "He who guards his mouth preserves his life: but he who opens wide his lips shall have destruction."

- James 3:5-6: "The tongue is a little member and boasts great things. …the tongue is a fire, a world of iniquity. The tongue is so set among our members, it defiles the whole body, and sets on fire the course of nature [it disrupts and destroys the cycle of your life, cutting your life short]; and it is set on fire by hell." If you allow your tongue to be set alight by the fire of hell, your words will release that evil hell-fire, and it will destroy your health and your life, as well as hurt others.

- Psalm 34:12-13: "Who is the man who desires life, and loves many days, that he may see good? Keep your tongue from evil, and your lips from speaking deceit."

- First Peter 3:9-10: "He who would love life and see (many) good days, let him refrain his tongue from evil.…"

- Mark 11:23 says that you will have what you say, especially if you believe that what you are saying will come to pass. This will work in the negative as well as in the positive. So if you speak death you will have it. I've heard it said that Elvis Presley often talked about dying at age 42, and it happened just as he said! On the other hand, we can speak life. We can establish our faith in God's promises of long life by confessing them.

We should take our stand and declare: "I shall not die, but live, and declare the works of the Lord" (Psalm 118:17). When under pressure and attack, we can prevail as long as we keep control of our tongues, refusing to speak satan's words of unbelief and death, and holding fast our confession of God's words of faith and life: *"I will not die young; I will live long and fulfill my life and ministry."*

When bad things happen and we are feeling down, our flesh will want to say something negative, but that will only make things worse. Say nothing if you are in doubt, remembering that our words have power! Refuse to speak an evil word. Remember that if you have a bad thought or feeling it can have no power over you unless you take it and own it by giving it voice. I believe that if it is not spoken or acted on, it will die unborn. So don't be a fool and curse yourself! Take control of your tongue, and start praising God and thanking Him for working all things together for your good (see Romans 8:28). Confess the Word of God which is life. You choose life or death by the words you speak!

Matthew 12:35-37 says:

>...*Out of the abundance of the heart the mouth speaks. A good man out of the good treasure* [the Word] *of his heart brings forth* [into his life] *good things* [by his words], *and an evil man out of his evil treasure brings forth* [into his life] *evil things* [by the evil words he speaks]. *But I say to you that for every idle word men may speak, they will give account of it in the day of judgment. For by your words you will be justified, and by your words you will be condemned.*

KILLER 5: WORRY

Most people know that our mental state has a big effect on our health. Peace and contentment lead to long life, but worry is a constant and common danger to having a healthy mind and body. The world encourages covetousness, the sense of never having enough, which makes us restless. As we focus on our problems, anxiety builds up and we lose perspective, especially forgetting that the Lord loves us and is ready and willing to help us. The details and things of life get too important. Worry builds up, and we become stressed when we carry the cares and burdens of life upon ourselves, rather than giving them to the Lord, trusting Him to work it all out. Our minds are fragile and are not designed to carry these weights and pressures of life. Therefore if we carry them, they will wear us out and grind us down. Continual worrying will make us weary and cause an early death.

The antidote to worry is to meditate on how much God loves and cares for us personally (see Matthew 6:25-34). By praising Him for His greatness and thanking Him for His goodness, we magnify God and then problems seem smaller. Knowing He cares for us gives us the confidence to cast all our cares on Him, as First Peter 5:7 says: "cast all your cares on the Lord, for He cares for you."

Consider these Scriptures regarding worry:

- Psalm 55:22: "Cast your burden on the Lord [releasing the whole weight of it onto Him] and He will sustain you...."

- Psalm 37:5: Commit your way to the Lord [roll and repose each care of your load onto Him], trust [lean on, rely on, and be confident] also in Him, and He shall bring it to pass."

- Proverbs 3:5-6: "Trust in the Lord with all your heart, and lean not on your own understanding; in all your ways acknowledge Him, and He shall direct your paths."

- Philippians 4:6-7: "Be anxious for nothing, but in everything by prayer and supplication, with thanksgiving, let your requests be made known to God; and the peace of God, which surpasses all understanding, will guard your hearts and minds through Christ Jesus."

The answer to worry is prayer. Instead of worrying, which is useless anyway, give it to the Lord in prayer. When prayer moves into thanksgiving, you know you have given it to Him, for you are now thanking Him for taking the burden from you and working on it. If you hold on to it yourself, then He can't help you; but when you give it to Him, you give Him the right to move on your behalf. The first thing He does is give you His supernatural peace, protecting your mind from worry and assuring you He is in control. In this way, believers can live with the constant inner calm of God's peace guarding our hearts and minds.

KILLER 6: PASSIVITY

It is well known that fighters with a strong will to live, will live longer. Passivity invites death. It is important for us to stay spiritually, mentally, and physically active. We saw in Chapter 7 that there is a spiritual battle over our lives and we must actively lay hold of God's life by faith, and resist satan's lies with the Word of God (see 1 Timothy 6:12). Paul is our example. He fought a good fight and laid hold of God's strength and life until the end, when he knew he had finished his course. His final words: "...the time of my departure [to heaven to be with the Lord] is at hand. I have fought the good fight, I have finished the race, I have kept the faith. Finally there is laid up for me the crown of righteousness..." (2 Timothy 4:6-8).

Spiritual passivity means we do not put up any spiritual resistance to sickness, tiredness, and the spirit of death. We become lazy, waiting for God to do something about it, rather than laying hold of God's promises of life and rising up and speaking His Word saying, "The Lord is the strength of my life. Lord, You are my Strength, You are my Healer," and then acting on it (acting as if it were true, which it is), for faith without corresponding actions is dead (see James 2:17).

Spiritual passivity means we are always giving in to our feelings. We don't feel like it, so we don't do it. As a result we never stretch ourselves or step out in faith. Yet it is facing new challenges and doing new things that keeps us young. Often it is only as we step out in faith and move into action, that new life, strength, and energy will begin to flow into us.

Spiritual passivity comes from become fatalistic, accepting everything that happens as the will of God: *"Whatever will be will be. I can't do anything about it. I don't have this promised blessing, because God must not have given it to me. If God meant me to have it, He would have given it to me."* This attitude is just a religious tranquillizer, that excuses failure and laziness. It is not biblical spirituality. Biblical faith works differently. God has already done all that He needs to do. Christ died to purchase every blessing of life for us, and then He poured them all out freely for (upon) us in the Holy Spirit.

Then He gave us His Word promising us that the blessing was ours, freely available for us to receive. Now we must be diligent in His Word, until we know it and are persuaded by it, and then we can come to Him in faith and believe we receive it (put our foot on it). Just as with Joshua and Israel, God has already given us our Promised Land, *but we must possess it,* or it will not be possessed. If we are passive and refuse to enter in, preferring to wait for God to do it, we will wander in the wilderness of lack and not enjoy a full and long life—but it will not be God's best and it will not be God's fault. It will be because we lacked diligence in seeking God and meditating on His Word, which results in a lack of faith to receive from God and a lack of courage to act on the Word.

God told Joshua that if he was diligent to meditate in His Word, then it would result in him being strong in faith (to believe the Word) and courageous to act upon the Word so that as a result, he would have good success in possessing the Promised Land (see Joshua 1:2-9).

Thus the promised blessings of God do not just fall on us while we are being passive. We must actively possess them by: 1) *knowing* the promise, by meditating on the Word, 2) putting our foot on it *(believing we receive it)*, and 3) *confessing* it with our words and actions. In faith we are to start speaking and acting as if the promise was true.

So when we know God's promise to give us life, we are to claim it and then start basing our words and actions upon it, rising up and doing what we thought we could not do before, saying, "Lord, You are my strength and my life today." As we take action, even though we may not feel like it, the life of God will start to become manifested in our bodies. Passive people are waiting for God to do something, but God has made His move, and He is waiting for us to do something!

God's best is for us is not waiting until we get sick and then receiving His healing—it is walking in divine health, daily drawing upon the life of Christ that is available through the power of the Spirit within us by faith (see Romans 8:11). This resurrection life has already overcome all sickness and death, so if we ask God to fill us with His life and health every day (our daily bread), we allow God's life to have dominion in our bodies. We will be covered by a shield of divine health, and we will develop a stronger immunity to sickness, stopping it before it can even get a foothold in us.

As well as being spiritually active in the Word and prayer, we must also keep our minds alert and active as we get older. A great trap nowadays is watching too much TV, for it makes us passive. It is much easier to do than, say, read a book, because that requires more effort on our part; but that mental activity is good for us, for it keeps our minds fit and strong. Having a hobby, project, activity, or interest outside our work is good for us and helps keep us mentally active and young.

One danger when people retire is that once the challenges and stimulations of work are removed, they have nothing else in their lives that keeps them active, so they quickly fall into passivity, and as a result they do not live much longer. Getting older does not mean that our mind has to get weak so that we lose our memory or have other mental problems.

Psalm 91:16 does not just promise us long life, but also that we will be satisfied with it. This means having a mind and body that stay in basically good health; for if we live a long life but lose soundness of mind, so that it does not function properly, then we would surely not be content and satisfied. So Psalm 91:16 includes the promise of maintaining our soundness of mind into old age. Settle now by faith that you will always have a sound mind. Say, "God has not given me a spirit of fear; but of power, love, and a sound mind" (see 2 Timothy 1:7).

We must also find ways to keep ourselves physically active as we get older. Although the activities we can do will change, it is vital to give our bodies some form of exercise, even if it is just walking, for otherwise it will go downhill faster. Staying active lengthens our lives.

POINTS TO PONDER

1. Six killers of longer life: foolishness; sin; unforgiveness; evil speech; worry; passivity.

2. Trusting in the toxic stimulations of alcohol, drugs, and smoking will kill us in two ways: 1) we are poisoning ourselves; 2) they make us passive.

3. By praising Him for His greatness and thanking Him for His goodness, you magnify God and then your problems seem smaller. Knowing He cares for you gives you the confidence to cast all your cares on Him.

4. When you know God promises to give you abundant life, claim it and then start basing your words and actions on it— rise up and do what you thought you could not do before.

Chapter 11

PSALM 91

Psalm 91 contains the greatest promises of divine protection and long life, as well as revealing the keys to how we can see these promises come to pass in our lives. Therefore in this final chapter, we will study Psalm 91 verse by verse.

1 He who dwells in the secret place of the Most High shall abide under the shadow of the Almighty.

2 I will say of the Lord, "He is my refuge and my fortress; My God, in Him I will trust."

3 Surely He shall deliver you from the snare of the fowler and from the perilous pestilence.

4 He shall cover you with His feathers, and under His wings you shall take refuge; His truth shall be your shield and buckler.

5 You shall not be afraid of the terror by night, nor of the arrow that flies by day,

6 Nor of the pestilence that walks in darkness, nor of the destruction that lays waste at noonday.

7 A thousand may fall at your side, and ten thousand at your right hand; but it shall not come near you.

8 Only with your eyes shall you look, and see the reward of the wicked.

9 Because you have made the Lord, who is my refuge, even the Most High, your dwelling place,

10 No evil shall befall you, nor shall any plague come near your dwelling;

11 For He shall give His angels charge over you, to keep you in all your ways.

12 In their hands they shall bear you up, lest you dash your foot against a stone.

13 You shall tread upon the lion and the cobra, the young lion and the serpent you shall trample underfoot.

14 "Because he has set his love upon Me, therefore I will deliver him; I will set him on high, because he has known My name.

15 He shall call upon Me, and I will answer him; I will be with him in trouble; I will deliver him and honor him.

16 With long life I will satisfy him, and show him My salvation."

Psalm 91 is a psalm of Moses, written during the dangerous forty years of wandering in the wilderness, describing the protection of God for those under the blessing—in contrast to Psalm 90, which describes life for those who lived under the curse because of unbelief. Psalm 91 is one of the greatest Bible passages promising divine protection to believers. It was a psalm that Jesus confessed, walked in, and fulfilled constantly. It talks about a secret hiding place we can always go to for rest and safety. It is vital we avail ourselves of this in these dangerous times. We must receive God's protection to live long enough to fulfill our mission in life.

THE SECRET PLACE DESCRIPTION

Verse 1: "He who dwells in the secret place of the Most High shall abide under the shadow of the Almighty" [the shadow of Shaddai]. This verse contains two parallel descriptions of this place. First, it is secret and Most High—unknown and inaccessible to the enemy. It is the place of the Most High—a high tower out of reach of the enemy. Later in Psalm 91 God promises: "I will set him on high [above and out of reach of the enemy] because he has known My name" (v14). In fact in verse 9 we see that this secret dwelling place is the Most High God Himself: "Because you have made the Lord, who is my refuge, even the Most High, your dwelling place." Psalm 32:7 says, "You are my hiding place; You shall preserve me from trouble; You shall surround me with songs of deliverance." And Psalm 27:5 says, "In the time of trouble He shall hide me in His pavilion; in the secret place of His tabernacle He shall hide me; He shall set me high upon a rock."

Second, it is protected by an impenetrable shield called "the shadow of the Almighty." This word *shadow* was used for a roof or covering that protected from the heat of the sun. It describes a covering of power, a spiritual shield. It is impenetrable because it is the covering of the Almighty, the Shadow of Shaddai—powerful protection!

The Lord is our shield: "You are my hiding place and my shield; I hope in Your word" (Psalm 119:114, see also Genesis 15:1; Deuteronomy 33:29; Psalm 3:3, 7:10, 18:2,30,35, 28:7, 33:20, 59:11, 84:9,11,18, 115:9-11, 144:2; Proverbs 30:5).

Another picture of this is a mother bird protecting its young under her wings: "He shall cover you with His feathers, and under His wings you shall take refuge" (Psalm 91:4). She opens her wings offering strong protection for her chicks, but they must trust themselves under the shadow of her wings. They must enter the hiding place provided or else suffer destruction. God spreads out His mighty wings for us, but we must choose to come under their shadow (covering).

Verse 1 summarizes the message of the psalm—if you make the secret place your dwelling, you will be shielded from all the attacks of the enemy. Those who dwell in the secret place will find their whole life comes under God's shield. Divine protection is available to all, but is only effective for those who dwell in the secret place. It is up to us. The secret place is a place of intimacy, of communion with the Lord. As we fellowship with Him, we enter into the secret (intimate) place in His presence.

Psalm 31:20 says, "You shall hide them in the secret place of Your presence from the plots of man; You shall keep them secretly in a pavilion from the strife of tongues." Jesus talked about this in Matthew 6:6: "But you, when you pray, go into your room, and when you have shut your door, pray to your Father who is in the secret place; and your Father who sees in secret will reward you openly." He is saying that in prayer, we should shut everything else out and enter the secret place in the Spirit where God is waiting to meet with you. He will reward you with blessing and protection openly (in your outer life).

There is a secret place in God's presence—a place of intimacy with the Lord. It is inaccessible, high above and out of reach of the enemy. It is protected by an impenetrable shield. But it is up to us to dwell in it. *The promises of Psalm 91 are for dwellers in the secret place.* Dwelling there speaks of continual, consistent communion with the Lord. To dwell in this place means we make it our home, the place we always return to every day in our prayers, not a place to which we just make occasional visits. Home is a place of safety where you keep returning to for rest, relaxation, and strength. People have (secret) hiding places they like to go to relax (home or perhaps a favorite room) if they are stressed or afraid. Psalm 91 says that we should make God's presence our secret hiding place, our home. It's a wonderful place to live.

If we make it our home, our dwelling place, then the result will be that we come and abide under the continual umbrella of His loving and powerful protection—we shall abide under the shadow of the Almighty. We can live under the overshadowing of His power as we walk through a dangerous world, but it is up to us to put ourselves under God's protection and enter the secret place. We claim this promise in the Lord's Prayer when we pray, "Lead me not into temptation, but deliver me from the evil one."

Jesus walked by Psalm 91, living in the secret place. He often got Himself alone to pray and enter it. He claimed the promises of this psalm out loud—that is why satan tried to use it against Him (see Matthew 4:5-7; psalm 91:11-12). Knowing that Jesus walked by this psalm, satan used it to try to trip Him up by trying to get Him to misapply it.

Psalm 91 explains how Jesus could walk through a murderous mob at Nazareth; how He could sleep in a storm, safe in His secret place; why those who were trying to kill Him were often unable to find Him. He died only when, in God's will, it was time to lay down His life, laying down His shield in order to die for us and for our salvation.

ENTERING THE SECRET PLACE

Verse 2: "I will *say* of the LORD, "He is my refuge and my fortress; my God, in Him I will trust." We enter the secret place by faith, by believing and confessing God's Word of promise. We must confess out loud the Lord as our shield and fortress. David, who was often in danger, did this continually as the psalms record: "The LORD is my rock and my fortress and my deliverer; my God, my strength, in whom I will trust; my shield and the horn of my salvation, my stronghold" (Psalm 18:2).

You have to make it personal and say it boldly by faith. Say, "But You, O Lord are a shield for me" (Psalm 3:3). His protection is available to all believers, but we have to enter it by faith, by a faith that is not ashamed to speak. Proverbs 18:10 says, "The name of the Lord is a strong tower; the righteous run to it and are safe."

When the pressure is on, we need to turn to the Lord for refuge. We can run into Him and surround ourselves with His protection, by calling upon and confessing His name in faith. His full name is the *Lord Jesus Christ. Lord* denotes His total authority—both His loving covering over us and His dominion over all the forces of the enemy. *Jesus* means our Savior, Healer, Deliverer, and Redeemer from the curse and judgment, the One who makes us safe. *Christ* denotes He has power and anointing to save. So calling upon His name is to call upon His divine authority and power to save us, believing we receive His protection.

Declare: "Lord Jesus, I run to You. Please cover me. I hide myself in You. I call upon You to protect me. I enter into Your secret place. In You I trust. I call upon Your name, for You are my Savior and Deliverer. I declare that You are my Fortress, my Refuge, my Shield, my Strong Tower."

This is how we put on our shield of faith (see Ephesians 6:16). The names of the Lord cover all areas of our salvation. As by faith, we declare and confess His name over us, with thanksgiving, His protective covering will be increasingly manifested over us. Say, *"Lord, thank You that You are my Righteousness, You are my Shield and Fortress, You are my Healer and my Deliverer. Thank You, Lord, You are my Life and Strength today."* As we do this daily, we abide under the shadow of His wings in the secret place of the Most High. The Lord Jesus did this and so we certainly need to as well.

Psalm 91:9-10 confirms this. But first we need to correct the translation of verse 9 which is confusing as it stands. Psalm 91:9 literally says, "Because you 'O Lord my refuge,' you have made the Most High your dwelling place." This is referring back to verse 2: "I will *say* of the Lord, '*He is* my refuge.'" Therefore verse 9 should be translated: "Because you said: 'Lord you are my refuge,' you have made the Most High your dwelling place." In other words, he entered into the secret place by confessing that the Lord was his refuge. Verse 10 then describes the results of entering into the secret place of the Most High: "no evil shall befall you, nor shall any plague come near your dwelling."

See yourself surrounded by a shield of God's power. See yourself in the secret place under the shadow of His wings. This is already true in your spirit. We are "hidden with Christ in God" (Colossians 3:3) protected by the Almighty, risen with Christ and seated with Him in heavenly places high above all principalities and powers (see Ephesians 1:18-2:6). But our outward life also needs to be covered by the shield of faith. This happens as we believe and obey Psalm 91.

Next we see the benefits of living in the secret place, which include guidance, immunity, deliverance, miraculous protection, and angelic protection.

Guidance (v3a): "Surely He shall deliver you from the snare [hidden trap] of the fowler." Satan sets traps in our paths, including offenses, temptations, and distractions; but if we commune in the secret place, God will be able to lead us around these traps into safety. Praying in the Spirit will prepare us for the day and help us avoid the enemy's traps.

Immunity (v3b): "and [surely He shall deliver you] from the perilous [destroying] pestilence" [disease]. Therefore part of the shield that covers us is divine health. It is God Himself who shields us as we see in verse 4: "He shall cover you with His feathers, and under His wings you shall take refuge" [you shall trust]. God is compared to a strong bird who spreads out His wings for us to flee to safety. A mother bird does this for her chicks as an invitation for them to take refuge from the sun's heat, from bad weather, and from dangerous enemies. God says, *"I spread out My wings—come under My protection. If your enemies want you, they will have to go through Me first!"* But it is up to you to trust yourself to God and enter the secret place under the shadow of His wings. The consequences if you do not do this is involve great danger. In Matthew 23:37-38, Jesus says, "O Jerusalem, Jerusalem… How often I wanted to gather your children together, as a hen gathers her chicks under her wings, but you were not willing! See! Your house is left to you desolate."

Enter into the secret place of the Most High, and let His protection enfold and cover you.

Consider:

- Deuteronomy 32:11-12: "As an eagle stirs up its nest, hovers over its young, spreading out its wings, taking them up, carrying them on its wings, so the LORD...."

- Psalm 17:8: "...Hide me under the shadow of Your wings."

- Psalm 36:7: "How precious is Your lovingkindness, O God! Therefore the children of men put their trust under the shadow of Your wings."

- Psalm 57:1: "My soul trusts in You; and in the shadow of Your wings I will make my refuge, until these calamities have passed by."

- Psalm 63:7: "You have been my help, therefore in the shadow of Your wings I will rejoice."

Deliverance from Fear (v4b): "His truth [His faithfulness] shall be your shield and buckler." Strong protection for our hearts comes only through meditation of God's Word and faithfulness. In the secret place of the Most High we receive assurance and revelation of God's faithfulness and promises which guard our hearts against fear (for fear opens the door to the curse).

Protection (v5-6). Verses 5 and 6 say that we will be protected from all attacks, whether by day or night, whether secret (invisible) or open (visible), and therefore we will be free from all fear. "You shall not be afraid of the terror by night." We are delivered from fear when we dwell in the hiding place. This promises us that neither nightmares nor anxiety at night shall afflict us, for we know that God's shield is over us even as we sleep. "Nor [be afraid] of the arrow that flies by day." Enemy arrows such as evil words, curses, and gossip against us will all bounce off our shield, so we shall not fear them. "Nor [be afraid] of the pestilence that walks in darkness [invisible diseases], nor [be afraid] of the destruction that lays waste at noonday" [visible disasters].

Miraculous Protection in the midst of danger and destruction, where you would surely perish otherwise. Verses 7 and 8 say, "A thousand may fall at your side, and ten thousand at your right hand; *but it shall not come near you*. Only with your eyes shall you look and see the reward of the wicked." Declare: "Evil and destruction shall not come near me, for no weapon formed against me will prosper."

Example 1: Noah's secret place was the ark which is a picture of Christ—our hiding place from God's judgment. Only those in the ark were saved when judgment fell because they were shielded. The hiding place was available to all, but most did not feel the need until it was too late.

Example 2: The first Passover night when Israel was about to exit Egypt, they were instructed how to make their homes a secret place by applying the blood of the lamb. Those who by faith dwelt under the blood were safe from the destroying angel. Inside they ate the lamb (eating the body—a picture of communion with Christ), while those not in the secret place suffered destruction. God said, "When I see the blood, I will pass over you; and the plague shall not be on you to destroy you" (Exodus 12:13). Most think this means God was the destroyer and He would see the blood and move on, but it is better to see God as the Protector from the destroyer. When He said, "I will pass over you," it meant, "I will hover over you as a shield."

Exodus 12:23 says, "when He sees the blood...the Lord will pass (hover) over the door and not allow the destroyer to come into your houses to strike you." This is why it is called the *Passover* (see Exodus 12:27). The word Passover is used in this way in Isaiah 31:5: "Like birds flying about, so will the Lord of hosts defend Jerusalem. Defending, He will also deliver it; passing [hovering] over, He will preserve it" [and His people there]. He hovers over us spreading His wings over us to protect us. But to enter into this protection, they had to apply the blood. Now we apply the blood to our lives by our faith confession: *"By the Blood of Jesus, You are my Righteousness, my Shield, my Hiding Place, my Healer, my Fortress."*

All our blessings of the secret place were purchased by the blood, and our faith in these blessings is in essence faith in the New Covenant made in the blood (death) of Jesus Christ.

As we apply the blood by our confession of faith, He hovers over us and we come under the shadow (shield) of His wings, which protects us from the forces of sickness and destruction.

Psalm 91:9-10 gives us a summary. As we saw, a literal translation of verse 9 is: "Because you said: 'Lord you are my refuge,' you have made the Most High your dwelling place." The secret place is the Lord Most High Himself. It is high above all enemy power, in the Most High God. We see that the key to entering it is a faith that confesses who the Lord is to us. To the one who chooses to dwell there, a general promise is given in verse 10: "No evil shall befall you, nor shall any plague come near your dwelling."

We should confess: *"No evil shall befall me, nor shall any plague come near me or my dwelling. No evil will come near my home, and no sickness shall come near my body."*

(Verses 9 and 10 repeat and confirm the thought of verses 1 and 2.)

Angelic Protection (v11-12), especially from accidents: "For He shall give His angels charge over you [at least one guardian angel is appointed to you, for Jesus said in Matthew 18:10 that each child had an angel assigned to him and he does not leave us when we grow up], to keep [guard] you in all your ways [a bodyguard protecting you, not just when in prayer, but as you go about your activities]. In their hands they shall bear you up, lest you dash your foot against a stone."

Believe in the ministry of angels to you: "Are they not all ministering spirits sent forth to minister for those who will inherit salvation?" (Hebrews 1:14).

The verses in Psalm 91 promise angelic protection from accidents, but not from the results of deliberate acts of sin and stupidity—angels do not and cannot override your free will. Jesus often claimed Psalm 91, so satan, fed up of hearing Him confess and claim it for His protection, thought he could use it to trap Him. In Matthew 4:6, satan subtly misquoted these verses to Jesus to try and make Him do something foolish. We could paraphrase satan's words as follows, *"Okay, Jesus, You like Psalm 91 so much, why don't You jump from this great height and claim this promise of God, and so prove to everyone you are the Messiah?"* But he twisted the Scripture, changing "all your ways" to "at all times" (see Matthew 4:6 KJV). The psalm applies to the dweller in the secret place walking in God's ways, receiving protection from mishaps. It does not apply to all circumstances at all times, whatever you do. Satan's deception was: *"Do Your own thing, Jesus, and God will still have to protect you."* This event proves that Jesus often claimed Psalm 91 or it would have been no temptation.

Jesus had to walk by faith in the Word, as a man, in order to fulfill His mission. He walked in its protection, and could not be touched, setting us an example (at the Cross He chose to lay down His protective shield so that He could die for us and bear our sin and curse. He laid down His life for us).

Having described the ministry of angels, the psalm then goes on to describe our authority and power over demons in verse 13: "You shall tread upon the lion [the aggressive, intimidating side of evil] and the cobra [the manipulating, subtle, poisonous side of evil], the young lion and the serpent you shall trample underfoot" [cf Luke 10:19]. This is our victory over satan. We are far above. He is under foot. We should not be in fear of demonic powers; they fear us.

Finally God speaks in verses 14-16, personally confirming the promises of the secret place in case we are tempted to think they are too good to be true. Verse 14a says, "Because he has set his love upon Me, therefore I will deliver him." The word for love here means that he clings, joins, knits himself to God, this is the one who has wrapped himself by faith in the secret place of God's presence (cf. Deuteronomy 30:20). So this is saying: *"Because he fully trusted Me and has chosen to live with Me in the hiding place, therefore I will deliver him."* This is the third time that the way into the secret place is described (see also verses 2,9).

Verse 14b says, "I will set him on high, because he has [personally] known My name." His determination to spend time alone with God means he has come to know God and His character. And verse 15 says, "He shall call upon Me, and I will answer him (the promise of answered prayer). I will be with him in trouble [yes, we will still face troubles in life, but His presence and help will be with us in the trouble]. I will [also] deliver him [from trouble], and honor him." Not only will He be with us in trouble, but also He promises to deliver us out of the trouble and to honor us—turning that situation around for our good, according to Romans 8:28.

The final promise to those who abide in the secret place is a long, satisfying, and blessed life.

As I have quoted throughout the book, verse 16 says, "With *long life I will satisfy him* [satisfaction means an abundantly blessed life as well as a long life, and that you can keep on going until you are fully satisfied], and show [manifest, demonstrate to] him My salvation." This salvation includes healing, deliverance from early death, and a full, long life now; but it is not limited to this life, for He will also cause us to behold and receive an eternal show (demonstration) of His glory in heaven (see Ephesians 2:7)!

Psalm 91 says the key to long life is to dwell in the secret place, and we do this by clinging in faith to the One who is the Source of Life, saying, "Lord, You are my Refuge, my Fortress, my Strength, and my Life. I trust in You."

A CONFESSION OF FAITH BASED ON PSALM 91

I dwell in the secret place of the Most High
I abide under the shadow of the Almighty.
For I say of the Lord, "You are my refuge and my Fortress;
my God, in You I trust."
Surely He shall deliver me from satan's snares
and from dangerous diseases.

He covers me with His feathers,
and under His wings I take refuge;
I shall not be afraid of the terror by night,
nor of the arrow that flies by day.
I shall not be afraid of invisible dangers or dramatic disasters.
A thousand may fall at my side,
and ten thousand at my right hand;
but it shall not come near me.

Because I have declared: "the Lord is my Refuge"
the Most High has now become my dwelling place.
Therefore no evil shall befall me or mine,
nor shall any plague come near my dwelling.
It will not come near my body or my house!

For He gives His angels charge over me,
to protect me in all my ways.
I have authority over satan.
I will tread upon all the power of the enemy
and trample it underfoot.

Because I trust in God, He will deliver me,
and set me on high.
He will answer my prayers.
He will be with me in trouble and
deliver me and honor me.

With long life will He satisfy me,
and show (manifest to) me His salvation,
for He will deliver me from evil and an early death.

POINTS TO PONDER

1. If you make the secret place your dwelling, you will be shielded from all the attacks of the enemy—your whole life comes under God's shield. Divine protection is available to all, but is only effective for those who dwell in the secret place. It is up to you.

2. In the secret place of the Most High you receive assurance and revelation of God's faithfulness and promises that will guard your heart against fear (fear opens the door to the curse).

3. All your blessings of the secret place were purchased by the blood of Jesus and His sacrifice on the Cross—for you.

Appendix A

WHAT ABOUT MARTYRDOM?

In this book I have strongly made and proved the claim that long life is God's general will for the believer (see Psalm 91:16). I have done this so that your faith would rise to believe and receive this promise of God and boldly declare it over your life. However there is an important biblical exception to this general rule that needs to be discussed: *"Is it not true that many wonderful believers both before and after Christ have had their lives cut short by martyrdom?"* That is a valid question, which I will answer.

There are the persecuted Old Testament prophets as well as the New Testament martyrs starting with Stephen (see Acts 7, Acts 22:20), and including most of the first apostles, such as Peter whose death glorified God (see John 21:18-19), and Paul who knew it was time for him to lay down his life in God's will, having finished the course that God had set out for him (see 2 Timothy 4:6-8). There is Antipas, God's "faithful martyr" (see Revelation 2:13) and many millions more in Church history. Such martyrdoms were prophesied by Jesus Himself as being typical of the church age (see Mark 13:9-13; Luke 21:12-17).

There will also be many more martyrdoms in the Tribulation: "I saw the woman, drunk with the blood of the saints and with the blood of the martyrs of Jesus" (Revelation 17:6, see also Matthew 24:9). These martyrs are seen in heaven in Revelation 6:9: "When He opened the fifth seal, I saw under the altar the souls of those who had been slain for the word of God and for the testimony which they held." These are resurrected at Christ's return in Revelation 20:4:

...Then I saw the souls of those who had been beheaded for their witness to Jesus and for the word of God, who had not worshiped the beast or his image, and had not received his mark on their foreheads or on their hands. And they lived and reigned with Christ for a thousand years.

Revelation 12:11 says of martyrs: "They overcame him [satan] by the blood of the Lamb and by the word of their testimony, and they did not love their lives to the death."

Are we saying that they missed God's will somehow because their lives were cut short? Certainly not! All these martyrs are highly honored by God for sacrificing their lives for the Lord Jesus. These all died for their faith in Christ and their testimony to Him, and moreover they did this in the will of God, for the Church grows from the seed of the martyrs. Martyrs die in the will of God, so that others can live. But as a result, God's promise of long life to them was not fulfilled.

How do we account for this? The supreme example of course is our Lord Jesus Himself, who was cut off in the prime of life, as a young man, as Isaiah 53:8 had predicted: "Who will declare [speak of] His generation [children]? For He was cut off from the land of the living." Yet it was the will of God for Him.

As a perfectly righteous Believer, Jesus had the right to have the blessing of long life and could easily have lived on for a long time without dying—actually because He had no sin, He could have lived on forever without dying. In fact, although they tried to kill Him on many occasions they could not, while He abided under God's protection. Even in Gethsemane He said He could call on the angels to protect Him, but did not because He chose God's will, which was to die for us. He died only because He laid His life down; it was not taken from Him. He voluntarily let His shield down and opened Himself up to death. He chose to die for us in order to take the curse (which includes early death) for us, so that we could have the blessing (including long life):

Christ has redeemed us from the curse [of sickness and early death], *having become a curse for us (for it is written, "Cursed is everyone who hangs on a tree"), that the blessing of Abraham* [which includes health and long life] *might come upon the Gentiles* [us] *in Christ...* (Galatians 3:13-14).

So Christ suffered a martyr's death; He laid His life down so that His earthly life was cut short. He did this in order to give us a long and abundant life. Thus His short life only confirms how much He wants us to have a long life. Christ having His life cut short does not contradict God's promise to us of long life, it actually makes it possible! He took the curse of an early death so that we could receive the blessing of an abundant, long life!

Jesus had the right to live long and could have claimed that right for Himself. But, He had a higher call from God—to lay down His life as a martyr for us. It was His right to have the blessing of long life, but instead He voluntarily laid down His rights and bore the curse of a life cut short for us, so we could have abundant life. He did it because it was God's special will for Him. God asked Him to make that sacrifice for us, and He made it; and as a result God rewarded Him with greater eternal glory:

> *Let this mind* [attitude] *be in you which was also in Christ Jesus, who, being in the form of God, did not consider it robbery to be equal with God, but made Himself of no reputation* [He laid aside His rights and life as God], *taking the form of a bondservant, and coming in the likeness of men. And being found in appearance as a man, He humbled Himself and became obedient to the point of death, even the death of the cross. Therefore God also has highly exalted Him and given Him the name which is above every name* (Philippians 2:5-9).

We are called to have the same attitude as Christ, that though we are children of God with covenant rights (to long life), we must be willing to lay aside those rights to do the will of God. Just like Christ, every believer has the covenant promise and right to long life, but God asks us all to follow His example and be willing to lay down our lives and our rights for the Kingdom and for others. Matthew 16:24 says, "Then said Jesus to His disciples, 'If anyone desires to come after Me, let him deny himself, and *take up his cross*, and follow Me'" (see also Matthew 10:38; Mark 8:34, 10:21; Luke 9:23, 14:27).

Therefore God asks certain believers to lay down their rights to a long life on earth in order for them to establish a witness for Him on the earth. Martyrdom has nothing to do with sickness, it is being killed for being a Christian and proclaiming one's faith in Christ. You can't make yourself a martyr. It is the highest honor God could bestow on you and it will result in greater eternal glory for you. It is the fact that you have a right to long life and yet you voluntarily lay it down that makes it such a sacrifice that God sees and rewards.

In Second Timothy 4:6-8, Paul demonstrates the attitude of a martyr:

> *I am already being poured out as a drink offering, and the time of my departure [to heaven] is at hand. I have fought the good fight, I have finished the race, I have kept the faith. Finally, there is laid up for me the crown of righteousness, which the Lord, the righteous Judge, will give to me on that Day, and not to me only but also to all who have loved His appearing.*

Therefore, martyrdom is a special exception to God's general will for our long life. He calls martyrs to lay down their earthly rights and lives to gain a greater heavenly glory and eternal life. Whatever they sacrifice for Him in loss of earthly life, He will multiply back to them in an abundance of heavenly life and glory.

Do you believe God's promise of long life? Do you know it is your covenant right? Are you willing to lay down those rights if He asks you and glorify God by a martyr's death? If He gave His life for you, should you not be ready to give up your life for Him?

Appendix B

LONG-LIFE SCRIPTURES

Genesis 6:3: "The LORD said, 'My Spirit shall not strive with man forever, for he is indeed flesh; yet his days shall be one hundred and twenty years.'"

Exodus 15:2: "The LORD is my strength and song, and He has become my salvation...."

Exodus 20:12: "Honor your father and your mother, that your days may be long upon the land which the Lord your God is giving you."

Exodus 23:25-26: "You shall serve the LORD your God, and He will bless your bread and water. And I will take sickness away from the midst of you...I will fulfill the [full] number of your days."

Deuteronomy 5:16: "Honor your father and your mother, as the LORD your God has commanded you [see Exodus 20:12], that your days may be long, and that it may be well with you in the land which the LORD your God is giving you."

Deuteronomy 11:18-21: "Therefore you shall lay up these words of mine in your heart and in your soul, and bind them as a sign on your hand, and they shall be as frontlets between your eyes. You shall teach them to your children, speaking of them when you sit in your house, when you walk by the way, when you lie down, and when you rise up. And you shall write them on the doorposts of your house and on your gates, that your days and the days of your children may be multiplied in the land of which the LORD swore to your fathers to give them, like the days of the heavens above the earth."

Deuteronomy 25:15: "You shall have a perfect and just weight, a perfect and just measure, that your days may be lengthened in the land which the LORD your God is giving you."

Deuteronomy 30:19-20: "I call heaven and earth as witnesses today against you, that I have set before you life and death, blessing and cursing; therefore choose life, that both you and your descendants may live; that you may love the LORD your God, that you may obey His voice, and that you may cling to Him, for He is your life and the length of your days...."

1 Kings 3:14: "If you walk in My ways, and keep My statutes and My commandments...then I will lengthen your days."

Job 5:26: "You shall come to the grave at a full age, as a sheaf of grain ripens in its [proper] season."

Psalm 21:4: "He asked life from You, and You gave it to him— length of days forever and ever."

Psalm 27:1: "The Lord is my light and my salvation; whom shall I fear? The Lord is the strength of my life; of whom shall I be afraid?"

Psalm 34:12-13: "Who is the man who desires life, and loves many days, that he may see good? Keep your tongue from evil, and your lips from speaking deceit."

Psalm 55:23: "Bloodthirsty and deceitful men shall not live out half their days; but I will trust in You" [for a long life].

Psalm 84:11-12: "For the LORD God is a sun [radiating health to us] and a shield [from sickness]; the LORD will give grace and glory. No good thing [including long life] will He withhold from those who walk uprightly. O LORD of hosts, Blessed is the man who trusts in You!"

Psalm 91:14-16: "Because he has set his love upon Me, I will deliver him; I will set him on high, because he has known My name. He shall call upon me, and I will answer him; I will be with him in trouble; I will deliver him, and honor him. *With long life I will satisfy him*, and show him My salvation." "I give

them life, long and full, and show them how I can save"
(Jerusalem Bible).

Psalm 103:1-5: "Bless the LORD, O my soul; and all that is
within me, bless His holy name! Bless the Lord, O my soul, and
forget not all His benefits: who forgives all your iniquities, who
heals all your diseases, who redeems your life from destruction,
who crowns you with lovingkindness and tender mercies, who
satisfies your mouth with good things, so that your youth is renewed like the eagle's."

Psalm 118:17: "I shall not die [young], but [I shall] live [long],
and declare the works of the LORD."

Proverbs 3:1-2: "My son, do not forget my law, but let your
heart keep my commands; for length of days and long life and
peace they will add to you."

Proverbs 3:13-18: "Happy is the man who finds wisdom, and the
man who gains understanding; for her proceeds are better than
the profits of silver, and her gain than fine gold. She is more precious than rubies, and all the things you may desire cannot compare with her. Length of days is in her right hand, in her left hand,
riches and honor. Her ways are ways of pleasantness, and all her
paths are peace. She is a tree of life to those who take hold of her,
and happy are all who retain her."

Proverbs 4:10: "Hear, my son, and receive my sayings, and the
years of your life will be many."

Proverbs 4:20-23: "My son, give attention to my words; incline
your ear to my sayings. Do not let them [the words of God] depart from your eyes; keep them in the midst of your heart; for
they are life to those who find them, and health to all their
flesh. Keep [protect] your heart with all diligence [from bad attitudes and wrong beliefs, by putting the Word of God first],
for out of it spring the issues [forces] of [your] life."

Proverbs 9:10-11: "The fear of the LORD is the beginning of
wisdom and knowledge of the Holy One is understanding. For by
me [wisdom] your days will be multiplied, and years of life will be
added to you."

Proverbs 10:27: "The fear of the LORD prolongs days, but the years of the wicked will be shortened."

Proverbs 11:19: "As righteousness leads to life, so he who pursues evil pursues it to his own death."

Proverbs 12:28: "In the way of righteousness is life, and…no death."

Proverbs 13:3: "He who guards his mouth preserves his life, but he who opens wide his lips shall have destruction."

Proverbs 13:14: "The law of the wise is a fountain of life, to turn one away from the snares [traps] of death."

Proverbs 14:30: "A sound heart is life to the body, but envy [and hatred] is rottenness to the bones."

Proverbs 15:4: "A wholesome tongue is a tree of life, but perverseness in it breaks the spirit."

Proverbs 17:22: "A merry heart [the joy of the Lord] does good, like medicine, but a broken spirit dries the bones."

Proverbs 18:21: "Death and life are in the power of the tongue, and those who love it shall eat its fruit."

Proverbs 22:4: "By humility and the fear of the LORD are riches and honor and life."

Proverbs 23:7: "For as he thinks in his heart, so is he…."

Proverbs 28:16: "A ruler who lacks understanding is a great oppressor, but he who hates covetousness will prolong his days."

Ecclesiastes 7:17: "Be not overly wicked, nor be foolish: why should you die before your [proper] time" [full age]?

Isaiah 1:19: "If you are willing and obedient, you shall eat the good of the land" [which includes a long life].

Joel 2:25: "I will restore to you the years that the swarming locust has eaten."

Joel 3:10: "Let the weak say, 'I am strong'" [in the strength of God].

Matthew 6:33: "Seek first the Kingdom of God and His right-eousness, and all these things [of this life, including days] shall be added to you" [length of life shall be added to us].

Mark 11:24: "Therefore I say to you, whatever things you ask [such as long life], when you pray, believe that you receive them, and you will have them."

John 10:10: "The thief does not come except to steal, and to kill, and to destroy. I have come that they may have life, and that they may have it more abundantly."

Romans 8:2: "For the law of the Spirit of life in Christ Jesus has made me free from the law of sin and death."

Romans 8:11: "If the Spirit of Him [the Father] who raised Jesus from the dead dwells in you, He [God] who raised Christ from the dead will also give life to your mortal bodies through His Spirit who dwells in you."

Romans 8:32: "He who did not spare His own Son, but deliv-ered Him up for us all [to die on the Cross], how shall He not with Him also freely give us all things?"

Romans 10:12-13: "...the same Lord over all is rich [gives freely] to all who call upon Him [who ask Him for life]. For "'whoever calls on the name of the Lord [Jesus], shall be saved'" [all who ask in faith shall receive His life].

1 Corinthians 15:57: "Thanks be to God, who gives us [now] the victory [over death] through our Lord Jesus Christ."

2 Corinthians 1:20: "All the promises of God in Him [Christ] [including long life] are Yes, and in Him Amen, to the glory [manifestation] of God through us" [through our faith].

Galatians 3:13-14: "Christ has redeemed us from the curse of the law [which includes an early death], having become a curse for us (for it is written, "Cursed is everyone who hangs on a tree"), that the blessing of Abraham might come upon the Gentiles in Christ Jesus, that we might receive the promise of the Spirit through faith."

Psalm 107:1-2: "Oh, give thanks to the LORD, for He is good! For His mercy endures forever. Let the redeemed of the

LORD say so, whom He has redeemed from the hand of the enemy." The redeemed of the Lord should say, "I am redeemed from the hand of the enemy. I am redeemed from the curse of an early death."

Ephesians 1:3: "Blessed be the God and Father of our Lord Jesus Christ, who has blessed us with every spiritual blessing in the heavenly places in Christ."

Ephesians 6:2-3: "'Honor your father and mother,' which is the first commandment with promise: 'that it may be well with you, and you may live long on the earth'" (from Exodus 20:12; Deuteronomy 5:16).

1 Timothy 6:12-13: "Fight the good fight of [the] faith, lay hold on eternal life, to which you were also called and have confessed the good confession in the presence of many witnesses."

2 Timothy 1:7: "God has not given us a spirit of fear, but of power and of love and of a sound mind."

2 Timothy 4:6-8: "…the time of my departure is at hand. I have fought the good fight, I have finished the race, I have kept the faith. Finally, there is laid up for me the crown of righteousness, which the Lord, the righteous Judge, will give to me on that Day, and not to me only but also to all who have loved His appearing."

1 Peter 3:9-10: "You were called…to inherit a blessing: For he who would love life and see (many) good days, let him refrain his tongue from evil…" (from Psalm 34:12-16).

2 Peter 1:3: "His divine power has given to us all things that pertain to life and godliness…."

Hebrews 8:6: "…He is also the Mediator of a better covenant, which was established on better promises."

3 John 2: "Beloved, I pray that you may prosper in all things and be in health, just as your soul prospers."

Revelation 12:11: "They overcame him [satan] by the blood of the Lamb and by the word of their testimony…."

Appendix C

LONG-LIFE CONFESSIONS

- I will live and not die. I shall not die (young), but (I shall) live (long), and declare the works of the Lord. I will live long and not die young. I will live to a full age (see Psalm 118:17).

- God will satisfy me with long life and show me His salvation. I will live to a full age (see Psalm 91:16). Devil, I'm not going to die today, I'm not going to die tomorrow, I'm not going to die next week, I'm not going to die next year, I'm not going to die in 5 years, I'm not going to die in 10 years, I'm not going to die in 20 years, I'm not going to die in 30, 40, or even in 50 years. I will be satisfied with a long life.

- I will rise up and possess my Promised Land.

- I will fight a good fight and finish my course on earth.

- I will walk before the Lord in the land of the living. I believe it; therefore, I speak it (see Psalm 116:9-10).

- Thanks be to God who gives me now the victory (over death) through my Lord Jesus Christ (see 1 Corinthians 15:57).

- The same Spirit of Him who raised Jesus Christ from the dead dwells in me, and He shall also quicken and give life to my mortal body by His Spirit who lives in me (see Romans 8:11).

- Thank You, Lord, for freely giving me Your life. I receive Your resurrection life and power to work in me and renew my life and strength. The life of Jesus is being manifested in my mortal body.

- Christ has redeemed me from the curse of sickness and early death, having become a curse for me (for it is written, "Cursed is everyone who hangs on a tree"), that the blessing of Abraham (including health and long life) might come upon me in Christ (see Galatians 3:13-14). I have been set free from the curse. I have been redeemed from the curse, for Jesus took the curse for me. That means I am no longer cursed. No curse can come upon me, because I am blessed. I declare myself free right now. I am redeemed, I am delivered, I am free. God's blessing of health and long life is upon me now. Goodness and mercy will follow me all the days of my life. Thank God, I am redeemed. Thank You, Jesus, for setting me free and releasing Your life and blessing upon me.

- I am strong in the strength of the Lord (see Joel 3:10).

- The Lord is my strength and song, and He has become my salvation (see Exodus 15:2).

- The Lord is the strength of my life (see Psalm 27:1).

- God has not given me a spirit of fear, but of power and of love and of a sound mind (see 2 Timothy 1:7).

- Through Jesus I have an abundant, long life (see John 10:10).

- My mouth is filled with the goodness of God's Word, so my youth is being renewed as the eagle (see Psalm 103:5).

- It will be well with me, and I will live long on the earth (see Ephesians 6:3).

- God will take sickness away from the midst of me, and the number of my days He will fulfill (see Exodus 23:25-26).

- My days shall be multiplied, and my years increased (see Proverbs 9:11).

A CONFESSION OF FAITH BASED ON PSALM 91

I dwell in the secret place of the Most High.
I abide under the shadow of the Almighty.

For I say of the Lord, "You are my refuge
and my fortress; my God, in You I trust."

Surely He shall deliver me from satan's snares
and from dangerous diseases.

He covers me with His feathers,
and under His wings I take refuge;

I shall not be afraid of the terror by night,
nor of the arrow that flies by day,

I shall not be afraid of invisible dangers,
nor of dramatic disasters.

A thousand may fall at my side,
and ten thousand at my right hand;
but it shall not come near me.

Because I have declared: "the Lord is my Refuge,"
the Most High has now become my Dwelling Place.

Therefore no evil shall befall me,
nor shall any plague come near my dwelling.
It will not come near my body or my house!
For He gives His angels charge over me,
to protect me in all my ways.

I have authority over satan.
I will tread upon all the power of the enemy
and trample it underfoot.

Because I trust in God,
He will deliver me and set me on high.

He will answer my prayers.

He will be with me in trouble
and deliver me and honor me.

With long life will He satisfy me,
and show (manifest to) me His salvation,
for He will deliver me from evil and an early death.
I will see and experience God's salvation.

Appendix D

WHAT ABOUT BELIEVERS WHO DIE YOUNG?

This book teaches that God's general will for us is healing and long life. One common objection to this is that we know good believers and Christian leaders who died young or in middle-age due to sickness or accidents. How are we to understand this? If we are not careful, when someone we know, to whom we look up, dies young, it can hurt our faith and stop us believing in God's promises of long life and healing. So I offer these guidelines to help you handle these situations correctly when they happen.

1. Don't judge God's will from what happens in someone's life.

Just because something happens does not make it God's will. God wants all people to be saved through believing in Christ (see 1 Timothy 2:4; John 3:16; 2 Peter 3:9), but obviously not all are saved. If someone is not saved, we do not conclude it was not God's will for him to be saved. Likewise, if someone was not healed, we should not conclude healing was not God's will for the person. The only way to know God's will is from His Word, for He has revealed Himself perfectly through His Word; and God makes His will clear that He wants us to have a long and blessed life. Do not judge (test) the truth of God's Word, by a person's experience! Humankind's experience must be subjected to God's Word, not the other way round. It must be submitted under the Word, and not to be placed above it, for God's Word is faithful and true.

One of my favorite Bible teachers, from whom I learned a lot, went to be with the Lord before he was 50 years of age. I still honor and respect him, but that does not mean I believe that was God's perfect will for him. The last thing that a person of God would want is that his or her early death would impede our faith in God's promise for our healing. So do not compromise your faith in God's Word because of contradictory circumstances. To walk by faith is to walk by His Word rather than by what our eyes see. Our attitude should be: *"His Word is true no matter what happens. God said it, I believe it, that settles it."*

2. Don't blame God.

We may not always understand why some people do not live out their full life span, but whatever happens, don't blame God as if it was His fault. You should know better than that! God is always faithful to His promises. If there is failure, it is certainly not with God. There may or may not have been some obvious reasons when or where they may have opened the door to an early death. You don't know everything about people's lives and faith and the secrets of their hearts. That is a private issue between them and God, and God won't reveal them to you, for He respects their privacy.

One day all things will be revealed and all questions will be answered, but now we must trust God and His Word, even though we may not always understand why things happen the way they do. That is part of what living by faith means. And remember that God does not have to give an account to you; rather, you must give an account to Him!

3. Don't judge.

If people have health problems or fail to live long, it is not for you to judge them. This is unwise as you don't have the necessary information. God is their only judge. You cannot judge rightly by outward appearances. If you had to walk in their shoes and face the challenges and demands they had to face, how do you know you would have done any better? Don't focus on how well others have run their race, but rather focus on running your own race to the best of your ability. Build your faith and wisdom from the Word of God as best you can, so you can run your race to the end. If you are going to judge someone, judge yourself! In other words, mind your own business! That is, get your mind off other peoples' business and onto your own business. That is what the

Lord said to Peter when he inquired about what would happen to John and the length of his life:

> *Peter* [after the Lord had revealed to him about how and when he would die], *seeing him* [John], *said to Jesus, "But Lord, what about this man?" Jesus said to him, "If I will that he remain till I come* [even if he never dies], *what is that to you?* [It is none of your business how long he lives! That is a private matter between him and Me]. *You follow Me* [you should concentrate on fulfilling the will of God for your own life]*! Then this saying went out among the brethren that this disciple would not die. Yet Jesus did not say to him that he would not die, but, "If I will that he remain till I come, what is that to you?"* (John 21:21-23).

Focus on receiving and walking in God's life and health for yourself, and don't judge (or be discouraged by) those who have struggled or are struggling in that area.

About Christian leaders—people especially find it a test of their faith when a good leader fails to live out the full number of his or her days. Surely they were following God's will? Why did God allow them to die so young? Again the main answer is that it is between them and the Lord, and when all is revealed we will see that the Lord is not to blame. Some comments about leaders are appropriate to help you respond if this happens.

First, don't judge them, because leaders often face greater pressures, stresses, and spiritual attacks than others. Also, if they are not careful they get so caught up in the work of the ministry they are not really dwelling in the secret place, or they can push themselves too hard and not take enough rest, so they open themselves to sickness as with Epaphroditus in Philippians 2:25-30:

> *I considered it necessary to send to you Epaphroditus, my brother, fellow worker, and fellow soldier, but your messenger and the one who ministered to my need; since he was longing for you all, and was distressed because you had heard that he was sick. For indeed he was sick almost unto death; but God had mercy* [healing] *on him, and not only on him but on me also, lest I should have sorrow upon sorrow. Therefore I sent him the more eagerly, that when you see him again you may rejoice, and I may*

be less sorrowful. Receive him therefore in the Lord with all gladness, and hold such men in esteem; because [it was] *for the work of Christ he came close to death, not regarding his life to supply what was lacking in your service toward me.*

Being overly busy, preoccupied with problems, or tired from lack of rest and rhythm of life can cause leaders to fail to hear and heed a warning of the Spirit that would save their lives. Also, to whom much is given, much is expected. Because of their position, leaders walk a narrower path and they do not get away with what others can (remember how one sin ended Moses' life, preventing him from entering the Promised Land). Also, a leader may be strong in certain areas of the Word, but weak in others. Were they really believing, trusting, holding onto, and confessing God's faithful promises for healing and long life?

Be inspired by the positive teachings and examples they have set for you, but realize that only Jesus is perfect, so there may be areas of their lives (such as youth renewal and long life) where they have failed to receive the promises. So obviously don't use their lives as your example in those areas. Follow them only as they follow God's Word.

All believers who have died are now cheering you on to run your race of faith to the very end, by receiving God's promises and power to do His will. Hebrews 11 describes the heroes of faith—all the believers who have died and gone to heaven, having successfully run their race of faith and been faithful witnesses on the earth. Then Hebrews 12:1 says, "Therefore, we also, since we are surrounded by so great a cloud of witnesses, let us lay aside every weight, and the sin which so easily ensnares us, and let us run with endurance the race that is set before us."

A cloud is a technical term describing the mass of people watching the runners from above in the upper stands of the Olympic stadium. This says that these believers are in the grandstands of heaven cheering us on to run our race with endurance to the end and not quit early. So cast off any sin that slows you down and receive His grace to run the race!

A Prayer: "Lord, we thank You for Your promises of long life.
We thank You for dying young so that we could live long.
We believe Your Word and receive Your promise of long life,
so that we may glorify You and bear much fruit for You,
and fulfill Your will for us on the earth.

Thank You for giving us newness of life
and renewing our youth,
so that we can finish what You have called us to do."

A Confession: "I shall not die young,
but I shall live long and declare the works of the Lord!"

CONTACT THE AUTHOR

You can contact Derek Walker by email at
d.r.walker@talk21.com

P. 136   top 2 lines
138   GUIDANCE

Another exciting title from DEREK WALKER

GETTING HEALED
A Guide to Receive Healing
by Derek Walker

Good health is vital to enjoy life and fulfill God's will—yet we live in a sick world. For many Christians, healing is mysterious and vexing. They see healing as hit or miss, and so find it hard to trust God to heal them.

Getting Healed builds your confidence in God's Word, enabling you to receive God's healing. It will transform your whole understanding of divine health so you can walk by faith in the healing power of God. Jesus said:

Therefore I say to you, whatever things you ask when you pray, believe that you receive them, and you will have them (Mark 11:24).

Jesus always meant what He said. From careful research of the Scriptures and confirmed by testimonies of actual healings, Bible teacher Derek Walker gives you four key revelations necessary to successfully implement Mark 11:24 to get healed and stay healed.

Getting Healed gives you all the knowledge you need to consistently receive healing from God every day of your life! It leads you step by step into believing that you receive healing when you pray. This book is a great investment in your future health and well-being, as well as an excellent source to equip you to minster God's healing power to others.

ISBN: 978-88-96727-34-8

Order now from Evangelista Media
Telephone: +39 085 959806 • Fax: +39 085 9090113
E-mail: orders@evangelistamedia.com
Internet: www.evangelistamedia.com